Technology Business Management
from Theory to Practice

Dr. Klaus Fochler

Technology Business Management from Theory to Practice

Cost Management for Hybrid IT & Agile Delivery

ISBN 978-3-9821349-0-1

"Technology Business Management enables IT leaders to effectively communicate the value of their IT investments while controlling the costs for their hybrid IT landscape and agile delivery."

—Dr. Klaus Fochler

Contents

Dear Reader,

Medium and large enterprises with annual IT budgets in the tens to hundreds of millions of dollars spend a significant portion operating and maintaining existing IT landscapes, leaving only the remainder for technology innovations. While IT leaders cope with challenging hybrid IT scenarios and agile product developments, cost control becomes inevitable.

Technology Business Management (TBM) is a game changer for IT leaders. It offers a methodology to stay in control and to elevate IT organization to the next maturity level.

As an IT leader who masters TBM, you position your IT organization more effectively, knowing which parts of your value chain are competitive and where to engage external vendors. To your business partners, you present IT costs comprehensibly. You demonstrate how to leverage cloud services efficiently, taking full advantage of elasticity while maintaining close control over costs.

This publication shows how TBM works, bridging the gap between theory and practice. Learn how to:

- Build cost allocation models and calculate service TCO.
- Formulate better IT value propositions through cost transparency.
- Manage cloud costs and hybrid IT scenarios.
- Avoid cost spirals in agile product developments.
- Rationalize IT service and vendor portfolios.
- Become stress-resistant by “variabilizing” IT costs.
- Apply TBM insights to strengthen your leadership communication.

I will show you how TBM automation works with reference to the products of Apptio, a market leader in the TBM space. I have chosen a selection of their products for IT financial management, cost transparency, as well as the management of cloud costs and hybrid IT scenarios to explain how you can benefit from TBM.

My consulting firm, Dr. Fochler & Company, helps clients transform their IT operating model through TBM and IT sourcing. This publication demonstrates our commitment and expertise.

I would like to give my special thanks to Barry Whittle. Without his relentless revisions, this publication would not have come to place. Thanks to Sarah Vreugdenhil and Matthias Herberg for coordinating the project and clarifying key terminology. Todd Tucker provided the guiding vision for TBM, and I am most grateful for his foreword to his publication.

I would love to get your feedback. Please contact me at team@fochler.com.

Yours,

Klaus Fochler

What is Technology Business Management?

The discipline of Technology Business Management delivers agility to shift direction, allocates resources to keep pace with business value creation, and continuously optimizes technology investments to fund innovations faster than the competition.

The concept of Technology Business Management (TBM) was introduced through the original works of Todd Tucker[1], leveraging earlier concepts of IT Financial Management and taking them to the next level.[2] Today the TBM Council – with its 9.000 members including top IT leaders – curates the TBM methods and standards. TBM provides decision-making processes and serves as a management foundation for important digital transformation initiatives, including determining the TCO of IT services, controlling cloud costs in real-time, and effectively managing the cost of agile product development.

TBM injects sound principles of IT financial management and allows IT managers to run their IT organization as a business, elevating them to strategic partners with company leadership.

Elevating IT Organizations to the Next Maturity Level

Cost accounting classifies, analyzes, and allocates costs to control current operations and plan for the future.[3] Traditional cost accounting tracks costs over time, assigns costs to a specific accounting period, and allows for comparison of costs across accounting periods. One of its goals is to allocate costs to meaningful cost objects. IT organizations have IT services or IT products, which they provides to their customers and what customers can relate to. For simplicity, we will use the term IT services.

An IT organization's cost accounting practices determine its maturity level and its relationship with the company's management team. Simplistically, high-maturity organizations win—and low-maturity ones lose.

> **You can easily tell the maturity level of your IT organization: Do you calculate service TCO, control cloud cost in real-time, and master costs of agile product development?**

Low-maturity IT organizations do not defensibly account for the cost of ownership for each of their IT services. Business units see their IT charges as arbitrary and unfair. These IT organizations lack a solid cost accounting model. They use a shotgun approach, distributing costs over business units without consideration of individual consumption levels or the allocation of costs to different IT services along the IT value chain.[4]

As these IT organizations realize that their service pricing is indefensible, they fail to articulate IT value to business partners and cannot determine the cost of indi-

---

[1] Tucker, T., 2016
[2] Ryan, R., Raducha-Grace, T., 2009
[3] Wikipedia, Cost Accounting, 2019
[4] TSO, 2011, p.201

vidual IT services for either cost recovery or as a basis for pricing services for external customers.

Low-maturity organizations struggle with cost accounting of cloud services. They are overwhelmed by the operational details from their cloud service providers invoices. Absent a view into cloud cost drivers, they aren't able to compare between cloud and on-premises services. Attempts to tackle the challenge with spreadsheet-ninja skills is like fighting the tide—a losing battle.

Adoption of agile product development methods promises quicker time-to-value, but potentially spiraling costs. Backlogs of features and user stories push back release schedules and drive budget overruns.

TBM allows IT organizations to reach the next maturity level. Only then do they gain recognition from top management.

This book is for IT leaders aspiring to reach the next maturity level. TBM propels an IT organization towards a partnership with business leaders and away from being merely a cost center.

Mature IT organizations have a detailed understanding of their IT value chain. They accurately determine the TCO of each of their IT services and control the cost of cloud services and agile product development in real-time using meaningful KPIs. They evaluate IT budgets based on business impact—like any other line of business capital expenditure. They align financial management activities with IT services and business capabilities.

Most importantly, these IT organizations develop a transparent charging methodology based on the actual utilization of IT resources. Strong cost accounting capabilities allow them to provide IT services to external clients and set prices that recover costs—or to become a profit center with a P&L statement. They determine where they are competitive and which IT services they should source from the cloud and which they can offer more cost efficiently than other market players.

Essential Elements of TBM

TBM moves IT organizations to the next maturity level with a better understanding of their IT value chain and accurate allocation of costs. It provides a clear positioning of each IT service by distinguishing one IT service from another. The TBM taxonomy delivers organizational structure and supports efficient communication about IT matters, prescribing standardization to the complex world of IT.

Taxonomy: Classification of things to establish a common language and structure, so that everyone is talking about the same thing.[5]

You can assume the cost types that are involved in providing IT services (hardware, software, labor, etc.), but not the allocation breakdown by each service. Most hardware, software, and labor spend are first assigned to intermediate IT services–like precursors in industrial manufacturing. Examples of such intermediate IT ser-

[5] Wikipedia, Taxonomy, 2019

vices are infrastructure and platform services. The TBM Taxonomy provides a general reference to analyze an IT value chain, and thus is a good reference for cost accounting.

A cost model is another TBM element—it configures the flow of costs along the IT value chain.[6] This is where you determine how costs are allocated – for example, from infrastructure and platform services to the IT services provided to customers. Activity-based costing (ABC) is the preferred cost allocation concept.[7] ABC identifies activities in an IT organization and assigns the cost of each activity to IT services and IT products according to actual consumption.

The TBM cost model is a multi-dimensional data cube holding information from general ledger (GL) accounts, organizational units, activities and performance, IT services and consumption, and cost data. The model explains the flow of costs across the various units of an IT organization, the intermediate IT services, and finally to the business services that deliver value.

TBM cost models explain the flow of costs along the IT value chain and their allocation to individual IT services.

The TBM Model presents cost information, with context, in three layers.

- The finance layer presents costs as GL accounts (e.g., hardware depreciation or amortized software license).
- The IT layer presents costs in the context of the various teams who focus on specific technologies (e.g., teams specializing on data management technologies or network communication technologies but also in the context of lower-level IT services such as infrastructure and platform services that are utilized to build business services).
- The business layer presents costs in the context of business capabilities and business services (e.g., the capability to check-in passengers and its supporting check-in service).

How can you best steer your IT organization with the data in the TBM Model?

TBM defines metrics to measure cost in the context of success factors and to accelerate effective decision-making.[8]. The effective management of an IT organization requires such metrics to measure cost for performance, alignment of the IT service portfolio to the needs of the business units, or investment cost for IT-based innovations.

Metrics are the steering wheel of TBM. You cannot manage an IT organization effectively without measuring critical success factors.

An effective TBM practice requires automation, which can best be achieved through dedicated TBM software. The TBM software category is the next evolution level of a software category formerly referred to as software for IT Financial Management (ITFM).

The purpose of TBM software is to continuously collect data from various sources

[6] Tucker, T. 2016, p.74 f
[7] Staubus, G. J., 1971, Kaplan, R. S., Bruns, W.,1987
[8] Tucker, T., 2016, p.28

inside and outside of the IT organization. e.g., traditional cost accounting software from SAP, IT service management software from ServiceNow, cloud billing data from AWS, or Application Lifecycle Management software from HP. Data is not only loaded from these sources but also systematically cleansed and semantically aligned through transformation processes before being stored in a multi-dimensional data cube. TBM software covers the scope of typical business intelligence technology.

TBM software enables automation and IT Financial Management to shift from periodic to real-time analysis.

Consider TBM software as a business intelligence technology for processing IT cost, performance, and consumption data. It allows stakeholder-specific analysis and holds data on organizational units, business capabilities, and—most importantly—IT services. IT cost, performance, and consumption data are continuously collected and analyzed. TBM allows traditional ITFM teams to move to real-time analysis. It enables a shift from periodic to continuous ITFM.

Why do you need TBM?

TBM allows IT and business leaders to make the right decisions to execute their business strategy and transform their organization. TBM answers core questions:

- How do we fund IT-enabled business innovations?
- Which IT services can we more efficiently source from outside providers?
- What are the real costs of our cloud services?
- Where can we reduce our cloud costs without impacting our business?
- How do we closely monitor the cost of our agile product development?

Extending IT Financial Management

TBM extends traditional IT Financial Management (ITFM) practices. ITFM encompasses all capabilities for budgeting, accounting, variance analysis, and forecasting for organizational units. TBM expands these activities to IT services and products.

Budgeting is usually performed over the period of a fiscal year. When the fiscal year mirrors the calendar year you will most likely create the budget for the following year in the 3rd quarter of your current year. Through budgeting you plan future IT costs, including OpEx as well as CapEx.

Budgeting reduces the risk of overspend and ensures business unit charges and company revenues cover predicted IT spend. As you execute your plan, compare actuals to plan. This comparison mitigates overspend risk and improves budget prediction reliability.

Gauge your organization's cost efficiency through accounting. Accounting collects information on incurred costs and assigns them to cost centers and cost objects. TBM supports cost accounting at the organizational unit level and for IT services and products. Accounting results are used to:

- detect variances between your budget plan and incurred actuals,
- perform variance analysis,
- determine chargeback amounts for the business units, and
- improve future budget planning.

TBM helps detect the root cause of overspend with budget variance analysis to actuals. It increases accountability of budget owners.

Hold budget owners accountable by surfacing unexpected cost drivers. Track predicted annual budget variance by:

- Combining actuals incurred with the planned costs of the budget for the remainder of the year, or
- Extrapolate costs incurred at their monthly overspending rate for the remainder of the year.

The latter accepts that you will not be able to stop the root causes of the overspending.

Variance between budget and actuals indicates cost saving opportunities. Traditional ITFM practices usually fall short when there is a need to dive into cost structures by cost types, cost pools, and cost objects.

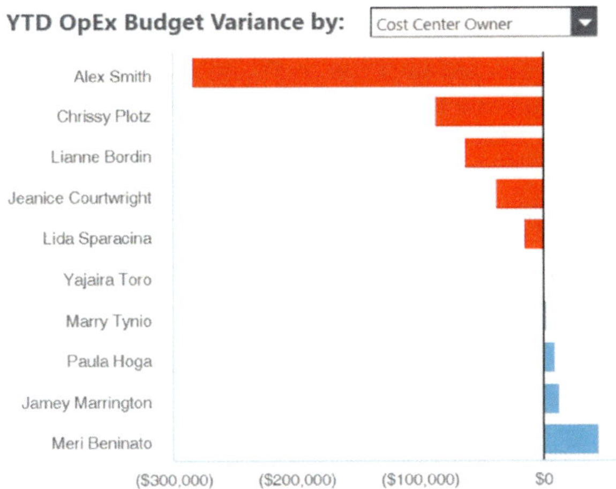

Diagram 1: Typical budget variance view by cost center owner [9]

TBM equips traditional ITFM practices not only with methods to plan and control costs but also to perform detailed variance analysis. TBM performs this analysis not only on the level of the organizational units but also for IT services and products. TBM helps to detect the root cause of overspend.

Determining Service TCO

TBM allows you to calculate the TCO of an IT service. We will refer to this as service TCO. Only then can you compare its cost and value and know whether you should continue to deliver the IT service with your team or better source it from outside service providers.

As Todd Tucker notes "when business leaders see the total costs associated with the services they consume, and they understand their role in balancing cost, quality, and consumption, they will tell you when the cost exceeds value." [10]

Why is it so hard to calculate service TCO?

Look at an airline check-in kiosk at an airport. We will categorize this kiosk as a business IT service. It's a check-in service. A passenger understands the check-in service. You present your travel information and documents; you are assigned a seat and issued a boarding pass. This check-in service is a cost object – an object to allocate cost to.

Let's assume the main cost types of the check-in service are hardware, software, and labor costs. However, we cannot immediately tell the portion of costs to the check-in service cost object. Follow the IT value chain, and you will find that most hardware, software, and labor isn't assigned directly to the check-in service. Often these are first assigned to intermediate IT services – like precursors in industrial

[9] Apptio, 2019
[10] Tucker, T., 2016, p.19

manufacturing. Examples of such intermediate IT services are infrastructure and platform services, e.g. IT services for client computing, containers, data management, application hosting, storage, etc. Following the IT value chain, you will find that the infrastructure and platform services are combined to constitute the check-in service.

Even an airline IT expert would struggle to list all infrastructure and platform services that constitute a check-in service. The architecture sketch in Diagram 2 is not all encompassing for a check-in service and lists selected architectural components only.

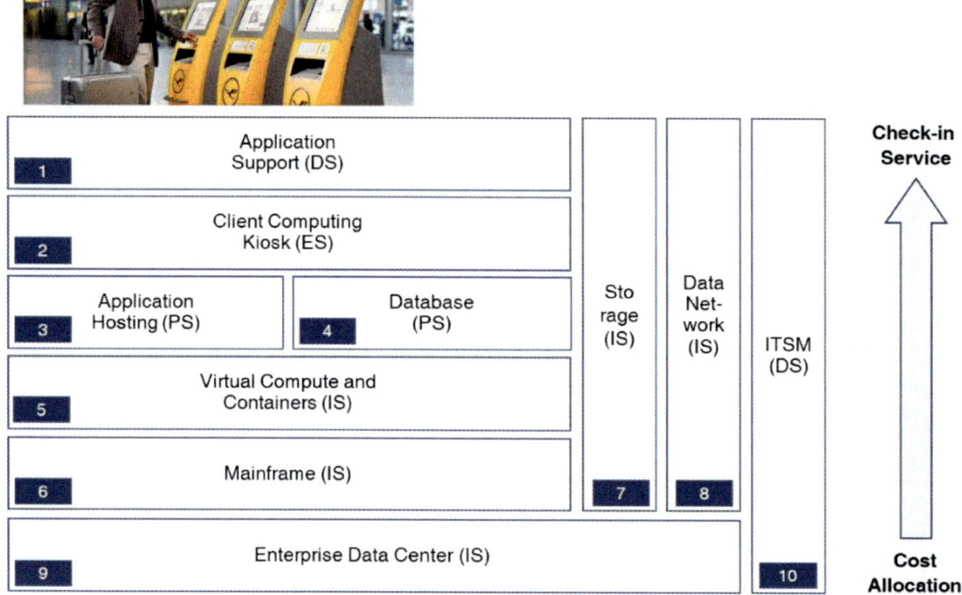

Diagram 2: Architecture sketch of a check-in service.

When dissecting the architecture of the check-in service while applying the structure of the TBM Taxonomy, we can distinguish the following intermediate IT services: [11]

TBM Taxonomy Service Types	Label	Intermediate Services
Delivery Services	DS	Application Support
		IT Service Management (ITSM)
End User Services	ES	Client Computing, Kiosk
Platform Services	PS	Application Hosting
		Database
Infrastructure Services	IS	Virtual Compute and Containers

[11] TBM Council, 2018, p. 15

TBM Taxonomy Service Types	Label	Intermediate Services
		Data Network
		Storage
		Mainframe
		Enterprise Data Center

Table 1: Intermediate services of the check-in service (example)

Most of the intermediate IT services not only serve the check-in service but other business services too (e.g., business services for crew management or aircraft ground handling).

So, the first hurdle you must take when calculating the service TCO of the check-in service is to understand its IT value chain. The TBM Taxonomy is a great starting point. Eventually, you will need to add a thorough understanding of the service architecture. Capture that by conducting interviews with IT architects or IT service managers – or as a more technical approach – by analyzing the CMDB.

Once you have understood the service architecture, build its TBM cost model. In the model, allocate cost from one layer of the IT value chain to the next.[12] Create the model layer by layer. Start at the financial layer with its GL accounts, group costs by cost type and cost centers[13] and finally to the various IT services, (e.g., the intermediate infrastructure, platform, delivery services as well as the check-in service).

Service TCO is calculated layer by layer along the IT value chain: Starting at the financial layer and up to the IT services.

On your path to calculate the cost of the check-in service, allocate the cost of the involved intermediate services to the check-in service.

If you allocate the cost to the check-in service wrong, business leaders may reach the wrong conclusions in running the airline (e.g., outsourcing the check-in business process to an external company vs. directly allocating funds to the business unit responsible for providing the check-in service).

Cost allocation methods utilize quantitative reference data (e.g., transaction counts, tablespace sizes, storage amounts, rack units) to achieve cost allocation aligned to causation. We will refer to it as data-driven allocation.

Data-driven cost allocation utilizes quantitative reference data, e.g., transactions counts to allocate costs in line with causation.

TBM determines service TCO by modeling the IT value chain of each service with data-driven cost allocations. TBM cost models are most effective when implemented with a dedicated TBM software solution built with graphical and tabular presentations and cost allocation strategies.

---

[12] Tucker, T., 2016, p.76

[13] The terminology cost center refers to a grouping of costs by organizational unit. The terminology is sometimes also used in a wider sense to describe an IT organization that only accumulates costs without aiming to generate a profit and receiving cost reimbursements from business units.

Controlling the Costs of Cloud Services

IT organizations need cloud cost management capabilities to reap the benefit of quick-to-deploy, scalable cloud services. Infrastructure costs for operating IT services on-premises are mostly predictable and dominated by CapEx; cloud costs are OpEx and mostly variable. Organizations need early insight into the drivers of their variable spend. Provisioning a cloud service is easy, controlling the costs of a cloud service is not. Configuration mishaps in the provisioning process surface as unexpected costs in a cloud bill—a wholly in-actionable piece of "insight" once the bill is in an organization's hands. Cloud instances that have been used initially by software development projects run idle and undetected as project timelines shift and teams undergo reorganizations.

Cloud services inject agility and can quickly scale IT operations. These benefits come with risks: Cost spirals, idling cloud instances, incomplete understanding of cloud service TCO.

The cost models for external cloud services are complex. The number of cloud service providers' IT services is overwhelming—the days when Amazon Web Services (AWS) and Microsoft Azure only offered traditional IT services for compute, data management, and storage are long gone. Their catalogues include IT services for virtual and augmented reality, artificial intelligence and gaming.

⊕	Amazon RDS Service (US East (N. Virginia))		$ 2484.45
⊖	Amazon RDS Service (EU (Frankfurt))		$ 3149.70
	DB instances:	$ 825.70	
	Storage:	$ 149.00	
	I/O:	$ 1785.00	
	Backups:	$ 190.00	
	Inter-Region Data Transfer Out	$ 200.00	
⊕	AWS Support (Business)		$ 563.23
Free Tier **Discount:**			$ -1.90
Total Monthly Payment:			$ 6195.48

Diagram 3: Calculation of the costs for the RDS IT service from Amazon [14]

Example: An IT service manages 50,000 user transactions a day. If each user transaction executes an average of seven I/O actions and these are also replicated to a standby RDS, then in one month of 30 calendar days this overall amounts to the following:

50,000 x 7 x 30 x 2 = 21,000,000 I/O actions.

Monthly cloud costs are determined by a number of parameters. For instance, the data transfer quantity and the I/O numbers for Amazon's Relational Database Service (RDS) impacts overall costs. Without accurate forecasting of these costs, it's

[14] Amazon, 2019

difficult to predict the TCO of cloud-based database services—setting up unpleasant and expensive surprises when IT organizations receive their monthly cloud bill.

Staying in control when managing cloud requires specialized tools. IT managers cannot evaluate the cost of cloud with just cloud service provider bills. They do not capture the fully-burdened cost of cloud.

Cloud service adoption needs additional management services from either the IT organization's staff or from 3rd parties providing cloud management services. Determining the TCO of cloud services is not only required during cloud adoption, but when controlling and managing cloud costs. The promise of cloud services is compelling, but you need a cloud management solution to keep you—and your cloud provider—honest about how successful the promise is being kept.

Most cloud services are commodities, and providers compete over price, adjusting their pricing models frequently. IT leaders have always struggled to control costs and communicate benefit, and the cloud-driven shift from CapEx to OpEx accentuates the challenge of waste, overspend, and unrealized ROI from cloud migration projects.

Financial management through spreadsheets is hard enough in the traditional operating model, but spreadsheets are overwhelmed by the complexity of cloud-focused operating models with per-second billing and variable discount structures.

Cloud bill complexity complicates data-driven decision making. Thousands of rows of cost data, 600+ evolving services from a singular cloud vendor, changing discount structures, on-premises-to-cloud mapping, reconciliation and allocation of costs: all push the limits of most IT organizations' legacy cost management solutions. Aggregated spend, performance, and utilization data across on-premise and cloud services further the disconnect between spend identified on a general ledger and the business outcomes. This fuels the perception that IT organizations are black boxes and not good stewards of capital.

TBM is essential to control cloud costs. IT organizations applying traditional mechanisms to manage cloud-enabled IT value chains are easily overwhelmed by the complexity of this task.

Existing financial management practices are a poor fit for the hybrid IT landscape–and to determine the real costs of cloud. TBM addresses the challenge of managing and controlling cloud costs by:

- Automatically ingesting, aggregating, normalizing cost data from multiple cloud service providers.
- Identifying anomalies for proactive optimization recommendations.
- Calculating the fully-burdened cost of cloud services (e.g., inclusive of IT service management).
- Providing like-for-like comparisons between cloud and on-prem solutions.
- Allocating cloud costs to the IT services consumed and recognized by the business units.

TBM is essential for IT organizations shifting direction, adding agility, and scaling operations with cloud services. IT organizations become overwhelmed by the complexity of cloud-enabled IT value chains when trying to control costs with traditional cost accounting software.

Managing Economics in Agile Product Development

IT product development has shifted from a waterfall to an agile delivery approach. The agile approach allows for a shorter time-to-market, and better addresses customer needs. Product enhancements in small, iterative increments embeds customer feedback into the development process.

The waterfall approach is the traditional development approach. It steers product delivery with a defined scope, agreed timelines and an approved budget. In this approach, you can't change one without impacting the others. Scope is defined by an evaluation of the costs and benefits of a product. The evaluation is based on the expected profitability. It is done prior to the start of the actual product development. A project is successful if it delivers the product scope within the agreed timeline and budget. IT organizations have spent decades delivering projects through the waterfall approach—a dedicated category of project management software supports it.

The waterfall approach has clear limitations. It is linear. The product value proposition and priorities can't change with market conditions. The value proposition agreed at the beginning isn't necessarily what's needed at the end. These risks compound.

The agile approach provides mitigation, and better alignment of product development to market conditions through faster and more frequent customer feedback. Commits to fixed iterations of work and the stable composition of teams allow flexibility to re-plan work. Inflight adjustments are crucial to the success of a product.

Many agile projects start with a minimum viable product (MVP). An MVP is a set of features that satisfy early adopters and which are at a minimum required in the product to provide some customer value. To get to their MVP, the scope is fixed, with time being the only variable. As the MVP must be released with a minimal set of features, its release date can get pushed. This first phase of an agile project is quite like a project following the waterfall approach for product development.

> **Agile product development employs a spiral-into-accuracy approach. IT and business leaders must regularly perform benefit-cost-comparisons to evaluate product economics.[15]**

After launching the MVP, teams switch to variable scope and enter the agile phase, open territory with product increments (PI) and sprints.[16] Each PI is defined by a number of sprints and each sprint has a constant duration and a stable team. Although costs are predictable per sprint, and per PI, they are variable over the entire product lifecycle (e.g., changes in priorities and product scope may require additional skill sets and resources). IT and business units can quickly lose track of a product's benefit-cost-ratio (BCR) as a product spirals into accuracy.

To keep track of required product features, agile teams maintain a backlog—a list of tickets describing desired product features and activities to deliver them. While

---

[15] Tucker, T., 2016, p.108

[16] Aljaber, T, 2019

it might be possible to score each backlog ticket for business value and to compare it to its one-time investment costs, it is hard to determine all subsequent maintenance, support and operation costs related to a specific feature. At the end of each sprint, organizations evaluate the costs of one-time invesments and yearly TCO against the benefits of the product. This delivers a repeatable evaluation of costs.

TBM accounts for the cost of an IT product and expected benefits. The comparison is required in both waterfall and agile delivery approaches. TBM verifies the BCR of agile and continuous IT product development against future maintenance, support, and operation costs. TBM foresees the integration with existing systems for project and portfolio management as well as application life cycle management. It delivers an all-encompassing view of investment and product lifecycle costs.

Who benefits from TBM?

TBM is a management discipline for forward-thinking IT leaders, who must:

- Master their IT value chain and related costs with detailed insight.
- Control the TCO of each IT service and the life-cycle costs of each product.
- Know which IT services they deliver more efficiently than market competitors (e.g., cloud or managed services)
- Successfully position their organization in the market field.
- Communicate meaningful KPIs on the cost and value of IT services

IT leaders who embrace TBM present the ratio of run costs to innovation investments. They shape the demand for their IT services and know which have a great BCR—and which do not.

These IT leaders explain to their company's CFO how to replace capital expenditure (CapEx) to operating expenditure (OpEx) by shifting existing IT services to the cloud. They assess their situation through KPIs and compare it with other IT organizations via benchmarks.

TBM does not only benefit CIOs and top IT leaders – their direct reports equally benefit. Business relationship and account managers identify IT services that drive up IT costs and initiate constructive discussions on the use of alternatives. They demonstrate investments in innovation projects and quantify the IT organization's innovation strategy.

They report on significant IT projects with up-to-date spend vs. budget reports, demonstrate the achievements of already invested budgets, and forecast the expected budget consumption until the end of a project.

Service and application managers receive an account of the consumed budget year-to-date and deduce future budget requirements through extrapolation and trend analyses. They capture the utilization of each IT service more effectively and identify which parameters impact IT service costs.

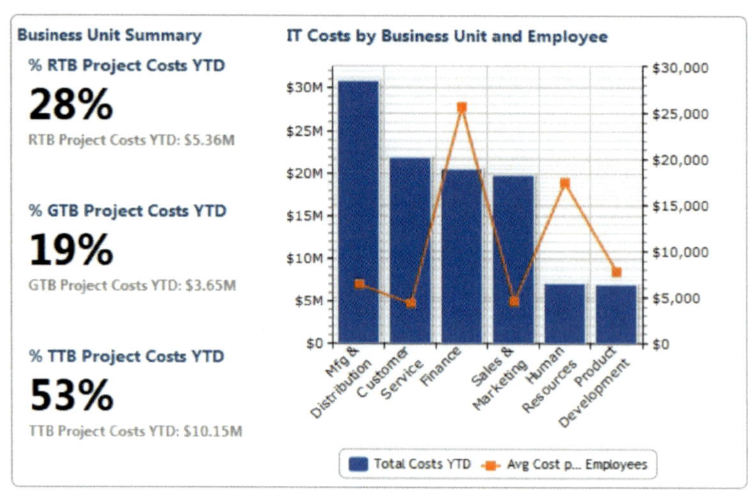

Diagram 4: Presentation of costs aimed at specific stakeholders.
IT project costs per business unit

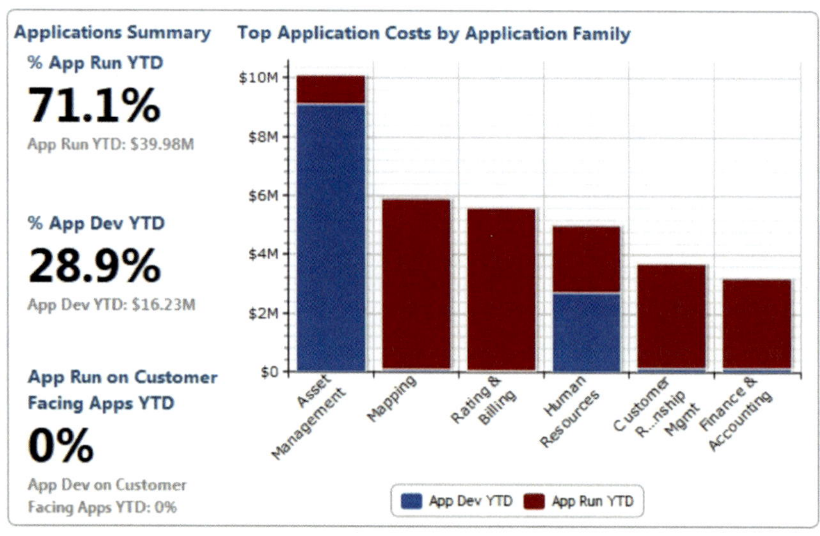

Diagram 5: Cost breakdown aimed at specific stakeholders.
Development vs. run costs [17]

IT operations managers quantify the consumption of technologies and capacities in monetary terms. They allocate costs to consumers, e.g., to infrastructure services for storage, network, and compute. As this IT function is typically responsible for the use of external cloud services, they restrict cloud sprawl, and unchecked cloud spend.

The TBM concept accounts for cloud service with dedicated objects in its taxonomy. It considers internal IT costs but also the cost of cloud services and associ-

[17] Apptio, 2016

ates them with all related internal costs and is thus fully capable of effectively managing hybrid IT scenarios.

TBM has been designed to control the cost of cloud services as well as internal IT services, thus making it suitable in hybrid IT scenarios.

IT Finance managers abolish their spreadsheets and avoid break-fix maintenance of hundreds of hidden and nested formulas. TBM provides insight into the IT value chain and an understanding of how costs flow from one IT service through to the next—and eventually to the business services. IT leaders become equipped with the right measures to break down IT costs by cost types, cost centers, and IT service as cost objects – all this with direct reference to the GL accounts and the data source systems. They calculate service TCO efficiently and achieve better business unit buy-in for consumption-based IT service charges.

TBM delivers real-time cost analysis. With dedicated TBM software, organizations pull cost and performance data from disparate source systems to build a standards-driven and defensible IT cost model.

"TBM brings the business translation to technological advances so you and your people can quickly decide on trade-offs and new investments to improve competitiveness, customer engagement, and the bottom line." [18]

—Mike Brady, Global CTO, AIG

Many more functions benefit from TBM than just the Office of the CIO. All core managing functions of an IT organization gain from better data, business-aligned cost allocation, meaningful KPIs, and automation.

[18] TBM Council, 2016

Getting You Equipped: Basic Principles of Cost Accounting

Cost accounting classifies, records, and allocates expenditure to determine the costs of services and products. It's the basis for creating TBM cost models to calculate the total cost of ownership of IT services and the costs of IT products.

IT leaders are not necessarily steeped in the specifics of cost accounting. If your career focus has "just" been on information technologies, we will get you equipped with the basics to master TBM.

TBM links the views of IT, business, and finance leaders. We can assume that finance leaders have an excellent understanding of cost accounting already. It's not much of stretch for business leaders either. TBM applies specific methods for cost accounting to IT organizations: IT leaders should attain a basic understanding of these methods so they can meet their finance and business peers on an equal footing.

We will explain cost accounting terminology and concepts that matter in TBM, and how to properly perform cost calculations for IT services and products. This section covers the six aspects you need to understand to create a solid foundation for your TBM journey:

1. Time-dependency: fixed vs. variable cost
2. Allocation complexity: direct vs. indirect costs
3. Three "Ws" of cost accounting: what, who, why?
4. Activity-based costing
5. Determining value

Time-Dependency: Fixed and Variable Costs

Costs are time-dependent. Fixed costs remain constant regardless of business activity – at least throughout a given time range. Variable costs are the opposite—they change with business activity. Commonly, we find both fixed and variable costs within the cost structure of an IT service.

When trying to determine whether a cost is fixed or variable, specify a time range. Look at your current accounting period. Does a particular spend commitment continue even if you stop delivering the IT service or project? If yes, you are looking at a fixed cost.

Examples of fixed costs include depreciation costs for hardware or data center buildings—even their rent costs in case of a long-term rental agreement which you cannot terminate in the short term. Even cloud services might be categorized as fixed costs. Reserved instances with a contract duration of up to three years as offered by AWS must be categorized as fixed costs.

> **When fixed costs characterize the cost model of an IT service, consuming less is like dieting without losing weight.**

Fixed costs inhibit financial agility and prevent IT leaders from giving business units choices for their IT consumption. Fixed costs do not disappear in the short term even when the business units use an IT service less. "Few conversations are more painful than when you tell your business partners that their IT costs didn't go down just because they used less." [19]

Consider fixed costs as sunk costs. Even if your company stops all activities, fixed costs will continue to hit you. Fixed costs tie up capital and operating funds when you need them most. Variable costs provide you with a different effect: They vary with consumption (e.g., external consultants). When business units use less of an IT service, they are charged proportionally less of the variable costs associated with the service. Variable costs are a useful lever to help shape business unit consumption.

IT leaders versed in TBM know the ratio of fixed to variable costs for each of their IT services. It is not enough to know the overall cost ratio between variable and fixed costs on the level of your organization only. That simply provides a high-level narrative, and not actionable insight per IT service. Determine the fixed to variable cost ratio per IT services and explain how much a decrease in service consumption lowers service TCO. This is crucial for business units looking to control spend through consumption choices. Education on how much they will save if they consume less of one service over another drives more informed IT use. IT organizations can perform root cause analysis of fixed to variable ratio outliers.

Determine the ratio of fixed to variable costs, then consider "variabilizing" your service costs to make your company more agile.

They derive strategies in preparation for a challenging business cycle. Economic downturns might require a quick reduction in service costs. This need for agility in the face of change is better served with variable rather than fixed costs. This cost structure is known as "variabilized" service costs. Determining the ratio between fixed and variable costs for each IT service is challenging. Recommended best practice? Tag cost items as fixed or variable when calculating service TCO.

Allocation Complexity: Direct and Indirect Costs

Cost accounting distinguishes costs that can be allocated directly, vs. costs that cannot be allocated directly to a cost object, such as an IT service. Direct allocation of costs to a cost object is only fair conduct if no other cost object has caused these costs. An example is cost of labor hours spent by a software developer on a specific project or for software licenses that have been purchased exclusively for a specific IT service and are not used by any other IT service.

Much more challenging than direct costs is indirect costs. Indirect costs can either not be directly traced to the different IT services or the complexity of attribution is deemed not worth the effort. Examples of indirect costs are costs for a data center or networking technologies. Their costs serve multiple IT services and cannot be allocated to one IT service only.

It is not an option to disregard indirect costs, just because their allocation to an IT service is complex. Both indirect costs and direct costs contribute to service TCO. To calculate service TCO, in addition to direct costs you must also consider a portion of the indirect cost that the service caused. Assign indirect costs in a way that is cause-related and transparent. Internal customers understand and accept chargeback when underlying assumptions are deemed fair.

---

[19] Tucker, Todd, 2016, p.180

While direct costs can be easily allocated to the cost objects that caused them, the indirect cost allocations must be based on certain assumptions. In a strict sense, it is more or less cause-related, but try to avoid an arbitrary process.

Defensible distribution of indirect costs is achieved through agreed allocation rules and identified cost drivers. Cost drivers determine the share of indirect costs per IT services. A cost driver reflects what causes, determines, or generates specific indirect costs. Allocations are made in proportion to what causes indirect costs.

> **Indirect cost allocation is at the core of each service TCO calculation. Allocation quality depends on how well an applied cost driver represents what causes, determines, or generates indirect costs.**

Here is an example: an intermediate infrastructure service providing storage to the airline check-in service as we described earlier. The storage service not only supports the check-in service but other IT services as well, such as the service for crew management. Its costs cannot be fully allocated to the check-in service alone —some is also assigned to the crew management service. These costs are indirect costs. An apt cost driver to allocate them could be the terabytes of storage consumed by the check-in service and the crew management service. Costs for the storage service costs are allocated to the crew management and check-in services in proportion to the amount of storage they consume.

Indirect costs become direct by elevating your perspective. Maybe indirect costs cannot to be allocated entirely to a cost object on a lower level of the IT value chain. Yet these costs may be direct costs at a higher level of the IT value chain when they can be allocated entirely to a cost object. We will explain this via another example: an intermediate infrastructure service for storage similar to the one that we described previously serves to two others intermediate services, such as a compute service and a database service. The terabyte consumed by each one of them is used to determine how storage service cost are allocated – just like we suggested for the check-in and the crew management service in the previous examples. Now, let us assume that these two intermediate services entirely serve a specific business service such as the check-in service. The costs for the storage service, which are classified as indirect costs to the compute service and the database service, then become direct costs to the check-in service. Though serving two intermediate services on a lower level of the IT value chain, these indirect costs can eventually be fully attributed to one service only at a higher level of the IT value chain – and become direct costs.

Impacts of Time-dependency and Allocation Complexity

After fixed vs. variable and direct vs. indirect costs let us now look at combinations of these categories and how they influence your options as an IT leader. We refer to these combinations as cost profiles. Some of them are of particular interest when managing an IT organization. Diagram 6 depicts possible cost profiles. Take a look at the quadrants in the upper right and lower left corners.

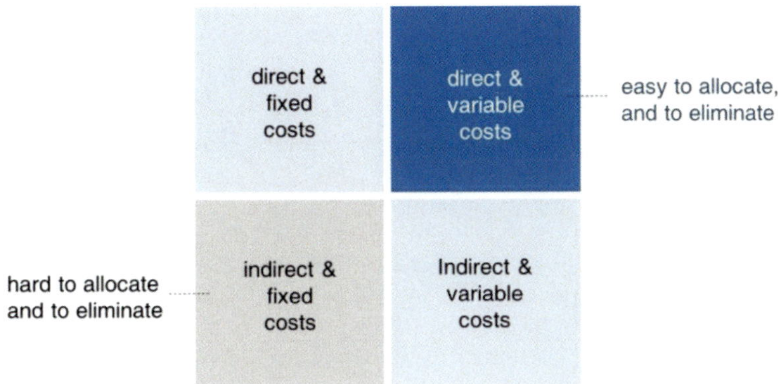

Diagram 6: Cost profiles as combinations of fixed vs variable and direct vs. indirect costs

The lower left corner depicts a cost profile that requires special attention: Costs are indirect and fixed, hard to allocate to individual IT services, and difficult to eliminate. Collectively they limit business agility. An example is the costs of a data center that you own and operate. If you shifted all of your on-premises IT services to the cloud, the data center depreciation would still be on the books for years to come – depending on the remainder of the overall depreciation period or on how fast you could sell it—impacting your company's profitability. With its costs being categorized as indirect costs, the IT services that moved out of the data center last would be carrying more and more costs while others who moved to the cloud first would not have to carry any of these costs any longer. This is a tough cost perspective to manage.

A better cost profile combines costs categorized as both direct and variable. They are easy to allocate and to eliminate, enabling the greatest business agility. An example is costs for business software that is provided as a service (SaaS) where the contract with the service provider allows a short notice period and service fees are charged per user. The yearly costs for such service may be higher compared to an on-premises installation and operation, but its costs are much easier to manage.

Three "Ws" of Cost Accounting: What, Who, Why?

Cost accounting is harder when discussing it with an international community. There are two global scale frameworks of financial reporting: U.S. GAAP, as promulgated by the Financial Accounting Standards Board, and IFRS, as enacted by the International Accounting Standards Board. Cost accounting methodology, and regulations in the USA for domestic, public companies (U.S. GAAP) differs from the way it is organized in other countries (IFRS).

Not only do different regulatory principles apply to accounting, the history and academic basis of cost accounting is different: For example in Germany – having the most complicated cost accounting methods in the world, as well as several other European countries – it is common practice to organize costs by cost types, cost centers, and cost objects, while in the USA it is common to only distinguish cost pools and cost objects.[20]

[20] Keys, D. E., van der Merwe, A., 1999

Diagram 7: Countries where adherence to IFRS is required for domestic, public companies [21]

TBM identifies cost pools, IT towers as well as IT services and products. Although originating from the USA, it is comparable to the German way of categorizing costs, by distinguishing what kind of costs incurred (pools), where costs incurred (IT towers) and why costs incurred (IT services and products). Irrelevant from which country and background you enter the TBM space, these are the three basic questions to answers:

- What kind of costs incurred?
- Where did the cost incur?
- Why did the costs incur?

Question	USA	Germany	TBM
What kind of costs incurred?	Cost Pools	Cost Type	Cost Pools
Where did the costs incur?		Cost Center	Cost Center, IT Towers
Why did the costs incur?	Cost Objects	Cost Objects	IT Services and Products

Table 2: Patterns of cost categorization

We will further elaborate on the categorization pattern that TBM uses. The lowest layer of the TBM Taxonomy starts with the GL accounts and then assigns cost to cost pools from there.

Cost pools categorize costs by the type of resources consumed. Costs incurred from consumption of the same resources or group of resources are allocated to one cost pool. It is a way of grouping costs at a higher aggregation level than on the rather detailed GL structure with dozens or hundreds of accounts. Examples of

[21] The IFRS Foundation, 2019

cost pools include costs for hardware, software, labor (internal and external), outside services or electrical power.[22]

From cost pools, TBM assigns or allocate costs to IT towers. IT towers categorize costs according to where the costs incurred, i.e., in which organizational unit of the IT organization. IT towers include technology functions acquired, supported, and delivered by an IT organization to provide its services and products.[23] Examples of IT towers are teams responsible for application development, support & operations, data centers, distributed computing, mainframe, storage, network, databases, communication, and end user technologies. IT towers also include teams responsible for project management (PMO), service management, security and compliance, service desk.

The IT towers build and support services and products. Services and products are the reason why IT towers exist. When allocating costs from IT towers to services and products you then face the challenge of allocating indirect costs for the first time as most IT towers do not deliver their work results to just one service or product alone. The trial continues as you follow the IT value chain over various intermediate services and products to the business services and products that are consumed by or delivered to the business units, external customers of an IT organization respectively.

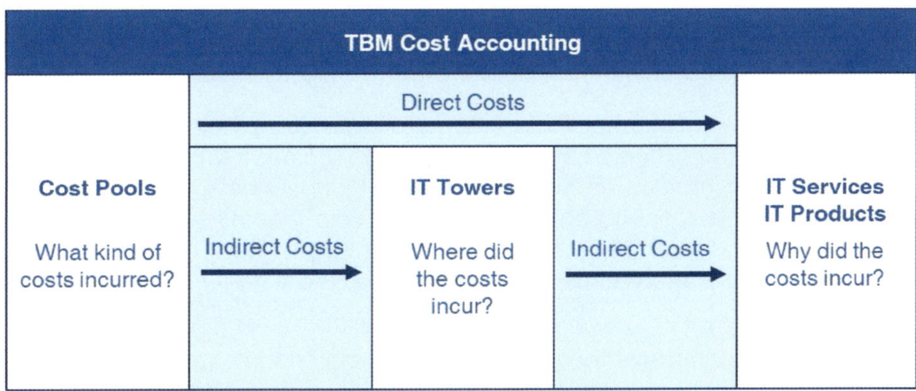

Diagram 8: Allocation of direct and indirect costs from cost pools to IT services and products [24]

The TBM concept generally shows the flow of costs in the following sequence:

- from cost pools to IT towers, and then
- from IT towers to IT service and products.

If your only goal is to determine service TCO or product costs, it is not required to route direct costs via the IT towers. You can allocate direct costs from a cost pool to an IT service or product directly.[25] In case you want to not only calculate service TCO or product costs but would also like to conduct cost analysis on your IT towers, you might want to consider routing even direct costs via IT towers first and then to

[22] Tucker, T., 2016, p.76
[23] Tucker, T., 2016, p.269
[24] Lindenthaler, B. 2008, p. 73
[25] Bragg, S, 2017

IT services and products. A set of academic publications elaborates on the pros and cons of either approach and on how they are applied in different countries.[26]

Indirect costs have to be allocated proportionally. It is good practice to first assign them to the appropriate IT tower and from there to the IT service and products. An example is the costs for the electrical power to operate your data center. They cannot be directly allocated to an IT service only and categorized as indirect costs. You first allocate them to an IT tower – in the TBM Taxonomy the appropriate sub-tower is labeled "Enterprise Data Center"—and to the IT services from there via an apt cost driver.[27]

Most IT costs are indirect costs. Therefore, the general allocation approach that TBM propagates—from cost pools to IT towers first and secondly from IT towers to IT services and products provides pragmatic guidance.

Effectively Allocating Indirect Costs: Activity-Based Costing

TBM suggests a method for the allocation of indirect costs that is known as activity-based costing (ABC).[28] It stemmed from the 1970s when the manufacturing industry went through a fundamental change with a significant increase in automation through robotics and computing. This boosted productivity dramatically and shifted costs from labor, which could in no small extent be directly traced to a product, to indirect costs for robotics and computers that were not immediately traceable to a specific product. Indirect costs started to dominate the cost structure of manufacturing.[29]

Until then, indirect costs (e.g., facilities, management, labor) were not dominant and mostly allocated to products based on labor or machine hours or other direct costs. Labor-intensive product carried more of the indirect costs. This approach wasn't suited for the increased portion of indirect costs that started to dominate manufacturing as automation consumed a more significant share of the total cost of production. Without a more cause-related method, the actual cost of products become distorted.

ABC was developed to improve the allocation of indirect cost. It promised to better process indirect costs with a more cause-related allocation. Instead of allocating indirect costs to products, ABC assigns indirect costs to manufacturing activities, such as cutting sheet metal. The cost of a product cost equals the sum of its activity-based costs. ABC assigns activity costs to the products demanding the activity. Cost allocation is performed over several layers of a company's internal process chain: First to sub-processes, and then to main processes, and finally to products. Its stepwise approach makes a distinction between preliminary, intermediate, and end products. Preliminary products are processed to become intermediate products and intermediate products become end products.

ABC ascertains cost drivers to break down and allocate indirect costs. These cost drivers are quantitative features that influence the costs of the processes. Indirect costs are broken down at the ratio at which the cost drivers occur in the individual processes or products.

---

[26] Krumwiede, K., Suessmair, A, 2007
[27] TBM Council, 2018
[28] Staubus, G. J., 1971
[29] Tucker, T., p.74

The changes that ABC introduced proved powerful. It not only allowed for a more accurate calculation of product costs by distinguishing activities, but also provided the levers for plant managers, engineers, and designers to change the cost of a product. Instead of making designs that were practical from an engineering point of view only, engineers could work more holistically, assimilating assembly costs within their designs and bringing down overall costs.

ABC gained a foothold in manufacturing because indirect costs increased, and today's correlation between indirect costs and productive machine hours or direct labor hours is rather weak. ABC works best in complex environments, where there are many machines, products, and tangled processes that are not easy to sort out.

Although ABC stems from the manufacturing industry, it has been applied in other industries as well. It is also a sensible choice for the cost accounting in IT organizations with their complex IT value chains and a significant portion of their costs being indirect costs.

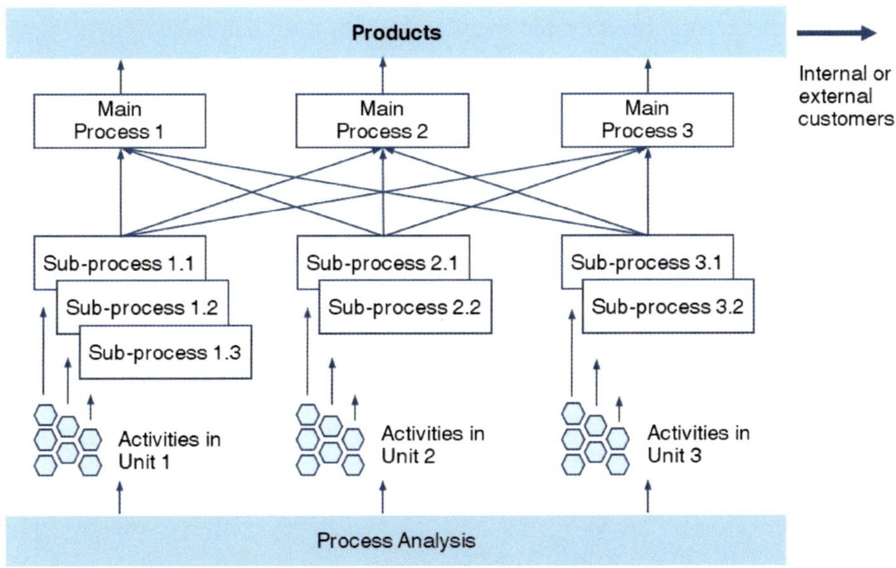

Diagram 9: Activity-Based Costing, schematic diagram.

You can apply ABC to calculating the costs of IT services and products. The IT value chain of an IT organization is just as much dominated by indirect costs as the manufacturing industry. An IT organization also uses a large variety of intermediate services which—as we follow the IT value chain—flow into other intermediate IT services or customer-facing IT services that are consumed by the business units. IT services that serve as a basis for further IT services can be compared to intermediate products while the customer-facing ones can be compared to end products in manufacturing. Each IT service represents a cost object, whether it is an intermediate or a customer-facing IT service.

IT services are organized in a cascade. On each layer of the IT value chain, one or multiple intermediate IT services may be combined and through manual work enhanced with added value to form another IT service. In a simplistic view, this cascade of IT services could be viewed as a hierarchy but in most IT organizations, it is instead a network of relationships with bilateral exchanges.

Just as applied in ABC, which allocates indirect costs to the individual corporate processes, TBM pursues the objective of allocating indirect costs to the individual IT services. This is achieved through cost drivers that best represent the cause of the indirect costs.

IT value chains of IT organizations are dominated by indirect costs. ABC targets a cause-related cost allocation by applying apt cost drivers.

Defining useful cost drivers seems challenging. But with a solid understanding of IT technologies this can be achieved:

- Costs for a storage service can be allocated to the downstream IT services based on the storage quantities assigned.
- Costs for a physical server infrastructure can be allocated to the operating system services running on them in proportion to the assigned CPU resources.
- Costs for a data center can be allocated to the infrastructure that is housed and operated in it in proportion to the floor space or the rack height units occupied by the individual servers.

The identification of right cost drivers lies at the core of ABC. An apt cost driver must quantify the cause of indirect costs. Finding appropriate cost drivers is vital to adopting ABC for TBM. It requires a solid understanding of information technologies and the activities to implement and support them. It is a task where IT leaders can play to their strengths. Without adopting ABC for the calculation of service TCO, the allocation of a large portion of the IT costs will be handled as a highly arbitrary process. If cost allocation is performed incorrectly, leaders in IT, business units and finance units can easily misjudge the company's situation when shifting direction during required transformation processes while continuously attempting to optimize technology investments.

Comparing Costs and Benefits: Is IT Worth it?

Calculating the costs of your IT services or products is a basis for sound decision-making—and the fuel for optimization efforts. But it is not sufficient. You need to also determine the benefits that your IT services and products provide. Only with costs and benefits can you determine the value of each of your IT services.

You can increase the value of an IT service by increasing its benefits, but also by lowering its costs. The option of value creation by fighting costs is easily overlooked.

Here is a simplistic formula to determine the value of an IT service or product:

$$value = benefits - costs$$

Cost transparency, i.e. a complete overview of all costs, is the basis for TBM. It is the key to all essential TBM analysis and decisions, both in running as well as in transforming IT organizations. Once the cost and benefits of an IT service are known, you know enough to determine its value.

You can then also conclude its BCR. It summarizes the overall value of an investment. The higher the BCR the better. If the benefit is higher than the cost of an IT service would seem to be worth it. But there is nuance here. What if other IT services have a better BCR and your human resources or cash flow to support them are limited? You have a choice. And possibly not one with a clear answer.

Let's look at how we can assess service benefits.

First a pragmatic approach: Calculate service TCO and confront customers with these costs as charges. If they reject it, you know costs are higher than the perceived benefit. This reaction, informative as it is, doesn't quantify what the perceived benefit actually is.

Benefits can be evaluated monetarily (e.g., increased revenues, cost savings) and qualitatively (e.g., customer satisfaction). The benefits of an IT service are typically determined before it is designed, built, and put into operation. It is part of a formal evaluation process to decide whether to approve requested budgets. The evaluation relies on financial indicators that describe an investment e. g., its net present value (NPV) or internal rate of return (IRR).[30]

Qualitative benefits also include the improved quality of a company's products or increased brand value. These benefits can be determined through surveys. They are also measured indirectly using operational indicators e. g., the availability of an IT service. Higher availability translates to avoided revenues losses, improved company image, or higher levels of work satisfaction among users.

But be aware: some IT leaders make extended reference to IT service management (ITSM) KPIs when trying to explain the value of their IT services. Examples include:

- number of incident tickets resolved or
- number of deployments of new software releases executed successfully.

Although assigning the value of IT services this way illustrates IT Service Management success, it falls well short of explaining the value of each IT service. Even the ITIL standard recognizes that "service management by itself does not provide any of the tactical benefits that business managers typically budget for".[31] ITIL suggests a measurement based directly on the benefit that the customer acknowledges in terms of positive effects on a company's performance indicators.

It is good advice to apply TBM with generally accepted methods of economic assessment, ideally based on hard dollars, Euros, or the currency that your company reports in respectively.

---

[30] Wikipedia,Net Present Value, 2019

[31] TSO, 2011, p.108

TBM Deep Dive

TBM is a supplement to other IT-standards such as ITIL and COBIT. TBM supports IT organizations offering IT services that enable business units to achieve intended business outcomes and growth. It does this through a framework of cost allocations to IT services and products—creating a basis for cost benefit analysis. TBM delivers sound management decisions during IT transformation processes and optimizes technology investments.

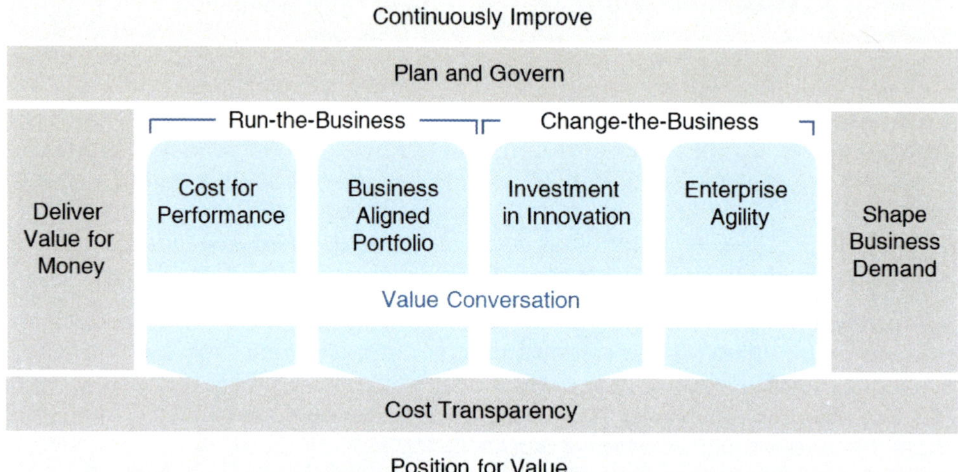

Diagram 10: TBM Framework [32]

The TBM framework distinguishes the organizational claims, disciplines, and value conversations.

Organizational Claims

- Continuously improve
- Position for value

Core Disciplines

- Plan and govern
- Create transparency
- Deliver value for money
- Shape business demand

Value Conversations

- Cost for performance,
- Business aligned portfolio,
- Investment in innovation,
- Enterprise agility.

Value conversations sit at the center of the TBM framework. TBM provides the

[32] Tucker, T., 2016, p.29

required cost information so that IT leaders and their business peers maximize operational IT efficiency in run-the-business spend (Run) and fuel IT investments to drive value in the company with change-the-business (Change) spend. Run capabilities view day-to-day business operations and determine a company's short-term success. Change capabilities enables medium to long-term success on the market. TBM supports a company's Run and Change.

Let us take a close look at the four TBM-infused value conversations IT and business leaders should have about running and changing the business.

Talk about Running the Business

Cost for Performance

The conversation on the cost for performance uses indicators to measures the efficiency in providing IT services at agreed service levels. This considers:

- amount of unused capacity in the infrastructure,
- extent of governance over external service providers,
- comparison of internal labor costs to its output, as well as
- cost-centric evaluations on IT service architectures to identify possible gold plating.

Business-Aligned Portoflio

The alignment of IT portfolios to business achieves two targets:

- rationalizing IT portfolios and
- shaping business demand.

IT leadership must determine the IT organizations portfolio of IT services and products. This includes as a list of business services visible to business units, but also intermediate IT services (e.g., infrastructure and platform services) often referred to as technical services. During this decision process, they rationalize their portfolios by identifying and eliminating redundant IT services (e.g., IT services for data management with similar capabilities).

Having defined the catalogues of business services and technical services, IT leaders look to shape demand. Knowing the total costs of services gives business partners a better understanding of the cost implications of their IT service consumption —and changes consumption patterns. If an IT leader holds business units accountable for the incurred costs via chargebacks, business units become conscientious consumers.[33] By disclosing the full costs of intermediate services to their IT units, IT leaders achieve the same effect on technical services.

IT leaders should provide business partners and internal IT units options with several versions of IT services that differ in quality and costs e.g., set service levels with varying support hours, service-level agreements, recovery time objective (RTO), recovery point objective (RPO), and reaction times in case of incidents.

The IT vendor portfolio should deliver risk mitigation (e.g., untying vendor dependencies) and increased purchasing power (e.g., reducing the number of vendors

[33] Tucker, T., 2016, p.149

and assigning large contract volumes to preferred providers).

Talk about Changing the Business

When looking back over the past decade IT organizations have started a remarkable transformation. It becomes visible in six aspects:

- Improving the financial foundation through strict IT budgeting, variance analysis and forecasting.
- Refining vendor management through classification, consolidation of contracts and control of vendor commitments.
- Organizing IT delivery in the form of IT services with attached service levels.
- Taking a clear market by publishing IT service catalogs.
- Adopting cloud services leading to a hybrid IT landscape with a mix of on-premises and cloud-based IT services.
- Turning themselves into service brokers.
- Changing their delivery paradigm for IT products from a waterfall to an agile delivery approach.
- Reducing the time-to-market for product enhancements through a DevOps methodology with automated testing and deployment.[34]

Many IT organizations are still in-flight of this transformation. Although challenging at times, this transformation is manageable when it is governed by TBM. The effects of this transformation impact into the business units with significant effects. They drive the speed of innovation and enterprise agility.

Investment in Innovation

TBM provides a framework to discuss innovation spend in IT services and products. Project spending is typically a small portion of the overall IT budget—often as little as 20%.[35] From the viewpoint of a business unit striving for technological innovation to improve business results, this can seem very low. The situation looks more dramatic when considering delayed IT innovation projects. McKinsey states that 33% of software projects with a budget of more than USD 15 million are delayed.[36] These delays frustrate business partners.

IT organizations reduce the costs and risks of project failure by including well-established IT services from outside vendors as part of their product innovation and then adding specific innovative features themselves. They then trade investment cost against future subscription cost for the outside IT services.

> **IT leaders who follow a smart innovation strategy buy the commodity and create innovation on top. It reduces investment costs, risks, and time-to-market.**

TBM allows the comparison of innovation options from a cost perspective and to

---

[34] Atalssian, 2019
[35] Tucker, T., 2016, p.168
[36] Bloch, M. et al., 2012

determine the break-even when trading investment cost against subscription cost for outside IT services.[37] TBM tracks the innovation spend of an IT organization compared with run costs. It can be sliced and diced, e.g., by IT service, business unit, time, or comparing fixed vs. variable costs. IT and business leaders can then discuss progress and determine future direction.

Enterprise Agility

The speed at which IT organizations move is subject to many discussions between IT and business leaders. Business units want IT organizations to react more quickly to new demand and respond faster to new market conditions. IT organizations have implemented IT services with cost structures heavily burdened by fixed costs, incurred by building applications, buying hardware, or signing long-term lease agreements for their data centers.

> **An IT organization will enhance a company's financial agility by "variabilizing" the cost structures of its IT services; that is by replacing fixed costs with variable costs.**

Fixed costs inhibit financial agility. They are largely considered a liability for a company as they turn revenue declines into significant losses. IT leaders transform fixed costs to variable costs through a process known as "variabilization". TBM maps the fixed costs of your IT services.

Once fixed costs have been identified and quantified, IT leaders build an action plan:

- Avoid assets that cause fixed costs and buy services with the required features (e.g., instead of buying high-performance printers, contract a printing service provider that provisions and maintains printers on-premises but charges per printed page).
- Replace IT services with a high percentage of fixed costs with SaaS offerings or cloud services from external vendors.
- Replace internal labor in selected areas with external labor – given that the new contracts include flexible termination options e.g., use external resources on "hype technologies" which are expected to have a short lifecycle and will soon disappear.

The hard part of the analysis is knowing the fixed cost percentage of each IT service. IT leaders that have not yet calculated service TCO will be challenged to determine the fixed vs. variable cost ratios of each IT service. TBM helps understand the cost dynamics of their IT services.

For IT leaders who are in the business of providing cloud services, the strategy will be drastically different. Cloud service providers carry significant fixed costs for building data centers and implementing hardware. This is part of their business model. As they carry capacity, they trust on their marketing and sales capabilities to sell their capacity as part of their service offering. They assume the fixed cost risk for their customers and thereby generate a profit. When demand for their cloud services drops, they are stuck with the fixed costs.

[37] Tucker, T., 2016, p.171

Explaining the TBM Taxonomy

The TBM taxonomy is built in layers which address the views of leaders in finance, IT and business units. The taxonomy distinguishes three views:

- Finance View: holds the lowest layers beginning with the general ledger and cost pools and sub-pools. Pools categorize costs by type.
- IT View: includes the layers for the IT towers and sub-towers. Towers are organizational units that focus on specific technologies or IT management tasks, such as servers, storage, networks, application development or IT service management.
- Business View: represents the highest layers of the taxonomy providing a generic set of IT service and linking them to business units and business capabilities. The TBM council currently works on the development of industry specific elements for these layers allowing for more meaningful reporting and comparisons within each industry.

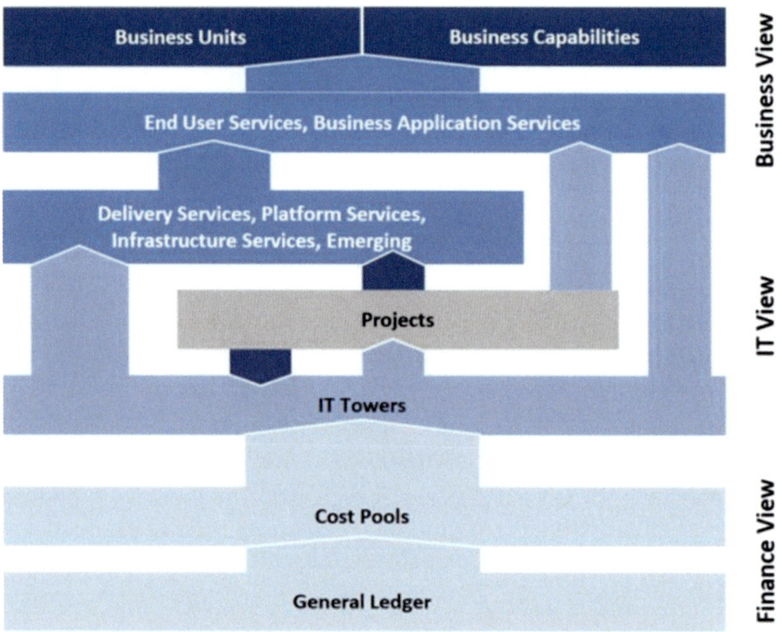

Diagram 11: TBM Taxonomy with typical cost flows [38]

The three TBM views link the worlds of financial accounting and the IT organization with their users and customers. Accountants find all details about cost types and cost pools, while IT service managers can find out more about the costs of their IT services.

Cost Pools

Cost pools categorize costs by cost type. The cost pools are distinguished by OpEx and CapEx Pools. The following table provides an extract of the TBM cost pools.

[38] TBM Council, 2018

It lists the OpEx Cost Pools. For a complete list of all TBM cost pools you should refer to the most current TBM Taxonomy publication of the TBM Council.[39]

Cost Pool	Cost Sub Pool	Explanation
Labor	Internal Labor	Costs for internal personnel (including wages, benefits and expenses).
	External Labor	Costs for external contractors (including travel and expenses).
Outside Services	Consulting	Costs for external consultancies charged per project.
	Managed Services	Costs for the management of IT services or applications by external service providers.
	Cloud Services	External public cloud services i.e., IaaS, PaaS, SaaS from external service providers.
Hardware	Expenses	Hardware expenses for spare parts, consumables or equipment below capitalization threshold.
	Lease	Hardware lease expenditures.
	Maintenance & Support	Hardware maintenance and support expenditures.
	Depreciation & Amortization	Depreciation and amortization of hardware capitalized on the balance sheet.
Software	Expense	Software expense of non-capitalized software purchases.
	Licensing	Software license expenditures for the use of non-SaaS provided software.
	Maintenance & Support	Software maintenance and support expenditures.
	Depreciation & Amortization	Software depreciation of capitalized software license purchases & software development efforts.
Facilities and Power	Expense	Data center space, power, security and other operating expenses
	Lease	Data center lease expenditures.
	Maintenance & Support	Maintenance and support services from external suppliers for the data center
	Depreciation & Amortization	Data center depreciation of facility build and leasehold improvements
Telecom	Expense	Voice and data network connectivity expenses including circuit and usage expenditures.
	Lease	Telecom lease expenditures.

[39] TBM Council, 2018

Cost Pool	Cost Sub Pool	Explanation
	Maintenance & Support	Telecom maintenance & support expenditures.
	Depreciation & Amortization	Depreciation/amortization of any capitalized telecom expenditures; typically, this will show up under Hardware or Facilities depreciation/amortization.
Internal Services	Shared Services	Miscellaneous shared services groups (e.g., HR and legal departments).

Table 3: Cost Pools and Cost Sub Pools [40]

IT Towers

IT towers are the organizational units, teams and departments respectively, that provide highly specialized expertise on individual technologies or IT management functions. These units include teams for database technologies, virtualization and container technologies, software development in Python or Java, IT service management, and so on. The members of these units deliver their work in support of IT services or products. Do not confuse them with the IT service or products.

IT services and products have specific properties and capabilities. IT services adhere to defined service levels in addition. Multiple IT towers deliver their expertise to make these IT service and products happen. In literature on management accounting, IT towers are sometimes more generically labeled as cost centers (refer to Table 2). The following provides only an overview of the TBM IT towers. For a more comprehensive list with all IT sub-towers you should refer to the most current TBM Taxonomy publication of the TBM Council. [41]

IT Tower	Explanation
Data Centre	Data Centers are purpose-built facilities to securely house computer equipment e.g., racks, cabinets, cabling, power, data connectivity, environmental controls including temperature, humidity and fire suppression, physical security and the people to run and operate the facility and its infrastructure.
Compute	Compute refers to both general and special-purpose devices and software that are programmed to carry out a set of arithmetic or logical operations. It includes a wide range of physical and virtual servers differentiated by platform and operating system. Examples are physical and virtual servers running a version of Microsoft Windows, Linux, Unix operating system.
Storage	Storage securely holds information and data to be retrieved later e.g., for application programs and code, databases, files, media, email and many other forms of information.
Network	Network includes the data and voice equipment along with the transport methods to connect systems and

[40] TBM Council, 2018

[41] TBM Council, 2018

IT Tower	Explanation
	people and to enable them to converse. Networks provide core connectivity within the enterprise data centers as well as connectivity to and access within office building and remote locations.
Platform	A platform is a group of technologies that are used as a base upon which other applications, processes or technologies are developed and operated.[42]
Output	Technologies for bulk printing and post-print processing
End User	Workplace technologies, mobile devices, end user software, printers, service desk and support services for end users.
Application	Business software as well as application development, operation and maintenance.
Delivery	IT operations center, IT service management, product/ program/ project management, account/ client management.
Security and Compliance	Information security, protection of personal information, disaster recovery
IT Management	IT strategy, IT architecture management, IT vendor management, IT finance—and TBM.

Table 4: IT Towers [43]

The IT towers are subdivided further into IT sub-towers. Diagram 12 shows an excerpt of this for some of the IT Towers.

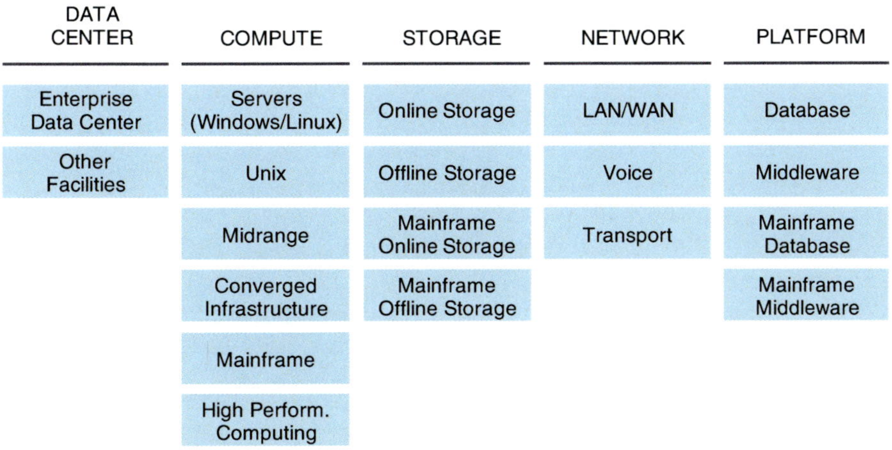

DATA CENTER	COMPUTE	STORAGE	NETWORK	PLATFORM
Enterprise Data Center	Servers (Windows/Linux)	Online Storage	LAN/WAN	Database
Other Facilities	Unix	Offline Storage	Voice	Middleware
	Midrange	Mainframe Online Storage	Transport	Mainframe Database
	Converged Infrastructure	Mainframe Offline Storage		Mainframe Middleware
	Mainframe			
	High Perform. Computing			

Diagram 12: Extract of the subdivision of IT towers into IT sub-towers [44]

[42] Techopdia, 2019
[43] TBM Council, 2018
[44] TBM Council, 2018

IT Services

An IT Service bundles technologies and labor. This bundle is more than the sum of its parts though. ITIL defines the concept of an IT Service abstractly as a "means of delivering value to customers by facilitating outcomes customers want to achieve, but without the ownership of specific costs and risks." The crucial factors are that the costs are determined in advance, and it is not the users of an IT Service who assume a warranty for the pledged features of the IT Service but rather the IT service provider. We want to explain the concept though the following definition:

> **IT Service: A combination of technologies and labor to generate a benefit to its consumers, offering specific features at a defined service level and at defined costs.**

IT services are created, operated, supported and maintained through the technologies and labor delivered by IT Towers, and potentially using other IT services (intermediate services).[45] This way an IT service can be refined and enhanced with additional technologies and labor to become a new IT service. IT services at the lower layers of the IT value chain are also known as infrastructure services or platform services. End-user-oriented IT services are known as end user services and business services. The aforementioned IT services are accompanied by delivery services, which are mostly characterized by labor (e.g. IT Service Management).

The distinction between IT towers as organizational units focusing on specific technologies and IT management functions and IT services might be confusing at first sight. IT services combine technologies and IT management functions. In particular they are guided by IT service management processes and delivered at defined service levels

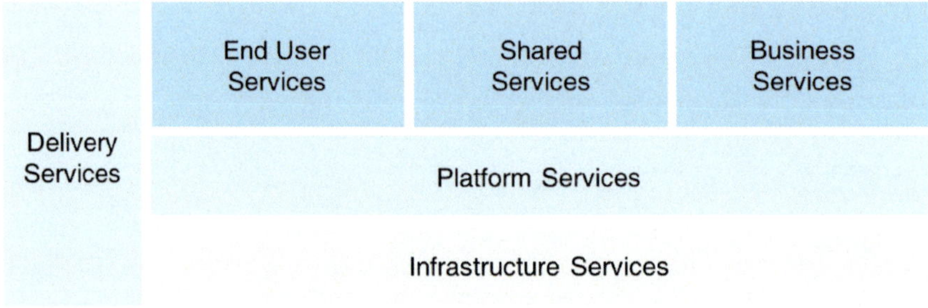

Diagram 13: Structuring of IT Services

Table 5 provides an overview of the IT Service categories suggested by TBM. For a more detailed list you should refer to the most current TBM Taxonomy publication of the TBM Council. [46]

Categories of IT Services	Explanation
End User Services	IT services that offer client computing devices, software and connectivity to enable users to access

[45] The technologies included in an IT service are supported by IT service management processes and delivered at defined service levels

[46] TBM Council, 2018.

Categories of IT Services	Explanation
	business applications; to communicate with other internal users, partners and customers
Business Services	IT services that offer business capabilities focused on a company's products and external customers to enable business units to win, serve, and retain customers. These capabilities are typically aligned towards a company's industry.
Shared Services	IT services that offer business capabilities which automate and support the organization's internal operations (e.g. HR, legal departments).
Platform Services	IT services that offer a base upon which other applications, processes or technologies are developed and operated e.g., for application hosting, database management, system integration.
Infrastructure Services	IT services that offer core and infrastructure capabilities and that are not typically directly consumed by users e.g., data center, physical and virtual server operating systems, storage, backup & restore technologies, data networks, load balancers
Emerging Services	IT services that offer new trending technologies in the market with limited adoption across the enterprise. The TBM council places services/offerings in the emerging services to provide visibility into possible future designation within the overall TBM taxonomy.
Delivery Services	These services build, deploy, support and operate the services listed above. This includes TBM, IT strategy development, governance, risk & compliance, enterprise architecture management, program and project management, software development, system integration, testing, IT service management, vendor management, IT security management.

Table 5: Categorization of IT services [47]

Developing a TBM Model

A TBM model controls the flow of costs and defines allocation rules to calculate the total cost of IT services and products. It drives costs along the IT value chain and across the different layers of the TBM taxonomy. Cost data is obtained from source systems via automated processes, undergoes syntactic and semantic transformation, and is first categorized in cost pools. From there it is allocated to IT towers, then to IT services and products. Eventually, costs are linked to business capabilities and assigned to business units as charges.

TBM is a cost allocation model. It is based on a standardized data model for cost types and cost objects within an IT organization. Its purpose is to enable business intelligence for IT costs.

[47] TBM Council, 2018

The TBM model sits on top of a standardized data model and assigns costs data to various entities of this data model. Its structure is typical for that of business intelligence (BI) applications. Business intelligence is the foundation of TBM. Just like in any other BI applications the data model supports stakeholders in business, IT, and finance units with specific cost data analysis and reporting.

The following diagram depicts an extract of a TBM model. It shows how cost gets allocated from IT resource towers to infrastructure services and then to business services.

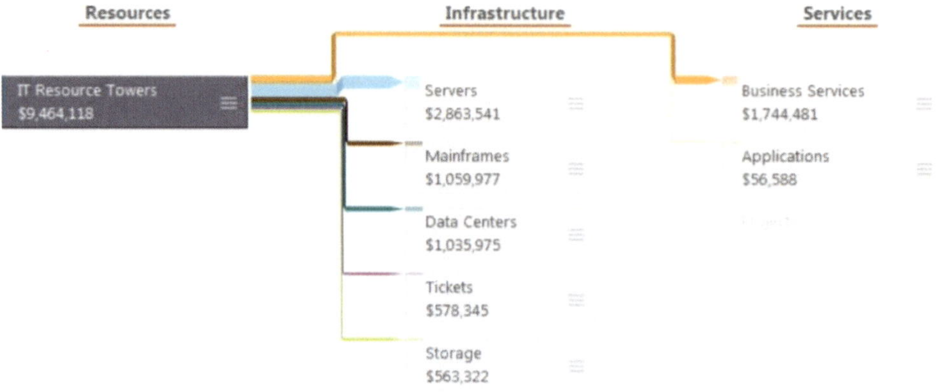

Diagram 14: TBM model [48]

Cost Allocation Strategies

The mathematics behind cost allocation does not have to be complex to be good. Allocation is easiest for direct costs which can be allocated straight to an IT service or product as cost object without having to split up the costs between different cost objects. Allocation mathematics come in play when having to allocate indirect costs. The most common allocation methods are the consumption based, weighted value and even allocation methods.

- A consumption-based allocation gets applied when the consumption of a cost pool or cost object by multiple downstream cost objects is known. Here is an example relating to the airline scenario that we introduced earlier. The check-in service and the crew management service both consume storage provided by the storage service. If we know how much terabyte (TB) of storage they consume, we can allocate the cost of the storage service proportionally. This consumption-based allocation requires quantitative consumption information for each downstream cost object.

Source Service	TCO	Capacity	Downstream Services	Consumed	Ratio	Allocated costs
Storage	$ 800	10 TB	Check-in	8 TB	0.8	$ 640
			Crew Management	2 TB	0.2	$ 160

Table 6: Example of a consumption-based allocation

[48] Apptio, 2019

- A weighted value allocation method is applied if such consumption values are not available. You then have to find an alternative allocation method that is as cause-related as possible. If you had not known the storage consumed by each downstream service in our example above, you could instead use the duration of the weekly full backup of the data for both services. You thereby assume that the backup duration is an indication of the data volume each service holds and thus the storage that it consumes. You could allocate the cost of the storage service proportionally to the back-up duration for each downstream service. This is called weighted value allocation. You can use this allocation method when there is no accurate consumption information for each downstream cost object, but there is a general knowledge on the distribution of usage. A special form of weighted distribution is an even distribution of costs.

Source Service	TCO	Capacity	Downstream Services	Backup Duration	Ratio	Allocated costs
Storage	$ 800	10 TB	Check-in	7 hours	0.7	$ 560
			Crew Management	3 hours	0.3	$ 240

Table 7: Example of a weighted value allocation

- An even distribution assumes that the costs of a cost object are evenly caused by the downstream cost object and thus can be allocated in this manner. It is fine to use this method if the assumption reflects reality. It is not fine to use an even distribution if costs are not evenly caused by the downstream cost objects and better cause-related cost drivers are available.

Source Service	TCO	Capacity	Downstream Services	Ratio	Allocated costs
Storage	$ 800	10 TB	Check-in	0.5	$ 400
			Crew Management	0.5	$ 400

Table 8: Example of an even allocation

More complex and less frequently used are recursive allocation methods and allocation methods based on complex formulas that take multiple parameters into consideration e.g., allocation of costs by the number of rack height units and electrical power consumed distinguishing when it is being consumed (day or night).

Table 9 compares the described allocation strategies by highlighting their strengths and weaknesses.

Allocation Strategy	Strengths	Weaknesses
Consumption based	• Supports acceptance for cost allocations by business units • Incentivizes behavior change, puts control in	• Can be challenging to collect the data • Data must be updated on a regular basis

Allocation Strategy	Strengths	Weaknesses
	hands of the business consumers	• Can result in swings or shifts in allocation percentages
Weighted	• Costs are based on actual use numbers • Allocations easily entered and understood • Puts control of costs in the hands of business units	• Actual utilization data may not be readily available
Even spread	• Easy to implement • Produces accurate grand total	• Does not fairly distribute cost based on use

Table 9: Comparison of selected allocation strategies

Diagram 15 shows how costs can flow across the different layers of a TBM model. Two types of allocation methods have been applied: weighted allocation (by user log-ins) and consumption-based allocation (by storage in use and labor hours).

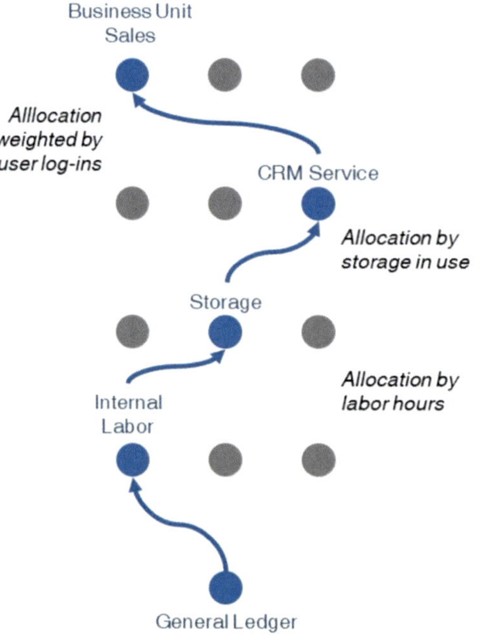

Diagram 15: Cost flow within a TBM model using weighted allocations [49]

[49] Apptio, 2014

Source Data

The source data for a TBM model originates from cost accounting applications e.g. SAP FICO or Oracle ERP Financial Management. Some cost information is directly acquired from external suppliers, e.g. the costs of cloud services from Amazon AWS or Microsoft Azure. Consumption data can be pulled in from IT service management (ITSM) or IT project portfolio management applications. Diagram 16 refers to the Apptio TBM product and depicts examples of TBM source systems.

Integration of the source systems and configuration of the data acquisition processes are essential prerequisites for operationalizing a TBM concept. It is steered through a transformation pipeline which handles missing data elements, normalizes data syntactically and semantically, and performs plausibility checks.

One important source is the IT service catalogue. Many IT organizations provide their catalogues via Intranet pages powered by collaboration technologies (e.g., Microsoft Sharepoint) or as a module in their internal web shops or ITSM suites. An IT service catalogue is not very dynamic. Changes to the catalogue typically do not occur frequently—at the most a few times per year. The automated loading of service catalogue information is not of prime concern. It may well be a manual loading process. The service catalogue information lays out the IT service landscape. It delivers the foundation of an encompassing TBM model. The service catalogue lists all IT services that an IT organization provides, and the cost objects costs are allocated to.

Diagram 16: Example of TBM source systems.[50]

A catalogue explains how intermediate and business services are connected. It provides details on service functionality, features, and service levels. Each service level constitutes a set of service qualities and timely goals such as service availability, RPO, and RTO as well as support times and reaction times in case of incidents.

An ideal catalogue must list the costs for provisioning and operations of each IT services. This is where most IT organizations are stuck. The costs published in

[50] Apptio, 2018

most catalogues do not reflect the true costs. They are not even guestimates. Determining the costs is a complex process. It's one of TBM's primary tasks.

Output

The regular and consistent (e.g. monthly) recording and allocation of cost data populates a multi-dimensional information cube: the TBM Cube. It is is an OLAP Cube with a data structure that allows fast data analysis along the dimensions that that TBM applies to maps IT services and products:

- cost,
- consumption,
- time,
- plan vs. actual.

The utilization of business intelligence concepts and technologies provides insights into the costs model for IT services and products, and ultimately supports the operational and strategic decisions to achieve corporate objectives. The TBM Cube is the basis for TBM assessments. Dashboards and reports present information in the form of meaningful key performance indicators (KPIs). The evolvement of information over time reveals adherence from actuals to plan and depicts trends for the future.

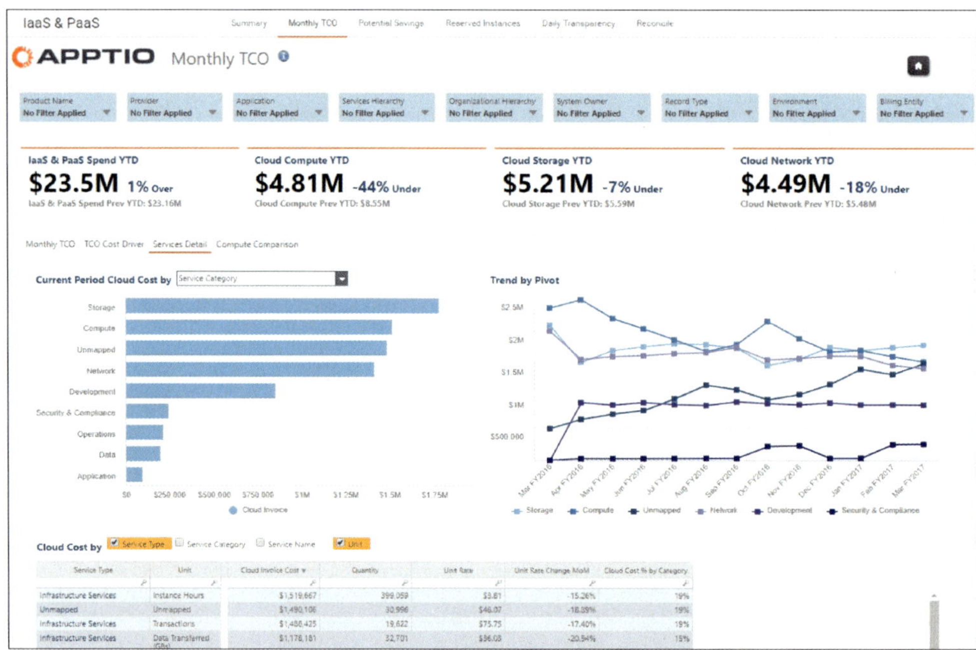

Diagram 17: Example of a TBM report [51]

[51] Apptio, 2019

Meaningful Metrics and KPIs

Regular measurement and reporting keeps you focused—use that information to make decisions and improve results. You measure through metrics. The most critical metrics are called key performance indicators (KPIs). The following tables list examples of metrics and KPIs for running and changing the business.

Metrics and KPIs for Running the Business

Metric/KPI	Category	Explanation
Service TCO	Costs	Allows chargeback and an indication for cost optimization opportunities.
Service TCO over time	Costs	Allows analysis on IT service cost drivers.
Actual vs. plan costs for cost pools and IT resource towers over time	Costs	Allows control and management of costs at the lower levels of the IT value chain during the budget year.
Unit costs for infrastructure and platform service	Costs	Allows cost comparisons to other IT organizations and cloud service offerings on the level of the infrastructure and platform services.
Customer/user satisfaction with IT services vs. ITSM costs	Benefits/ costs	Allows insight into the effect of ITSM cost on customer satisfaction. Customer satisfaction can be measured via survey results.
Service level achievements vs. ITSM costs	Benefits/ Costs	Allows measurement of the correlation between service level achievements and the cost of delivery service i.e., IT service management to identify improvement opportunities.

Table 10: Metrics and KPIs for running the business

Metrics and KPIs for Changing the Business

Metric/KPI	Category	Explanation
Cost agility: fixed-variable cost ratio of IT services	Costs	Allows determining financial agility and how a reduction in the consumption of individual IT services impacts short-term costs.
Actual vs. plan costs for IT products and projects	Costs	Allows close monitoring during product development and project delivery in order to enable early intervention and to counter with risk mitigation action.
Change vs. run costs	Costs	Allows determining the ratio of the investment into innovations and changes compared to the costs for maintaining the status quo.

Metric/KPI	Category	Explanation
Allocation of IT project costs mapped to company objectives	Benefits/ Costs	Allows an illustration of the significance of IT investments in achieving each of the company's objectives.
Cumulative net present value of the project portfolio	Benefits/ Costs	Allows measurement of the savings and additional revenue generated once the currently ongoing projects have been completed over a defined calculation period (e.g. 7-year lifespan of the project results) minus investment and run costs during this period.
Project benefits for business and IT units	Benefits	Allows responding to business unit's perception that insufficient IT project investments are dedicated to their benefit: "Is IT only concerned with its own affairs or does it actually change our business?"

Table 11: Metrics and KPIs for changing the business

A small survey published by the TBM Council illustrates the importance of selected metrics and KPIs from the point of view of IT managers.[52]

Category	Metric	Votes
Financial Foundation	IT Spend vs. Plan (OpEx & CapEx variance)	16
	Application and Service TCO	9
	Infrastructure Unit Costs vs. Target / Benchmarks	7
Delivery	% of Projects On-Time, On-Budget, On Spec	13
	% of Business-Facing Services Meeting SLAs	9
Innovation & Agility	% of IT Spend On Run, Grow, Transform the Business	14
	% of Project Spend On Customer Facing Initiatives	10
Business Value	IT Spend By Business Unit	11
	Customer Satisfaction Scores For Business-Facing Services	9
	% of IT Spend By Business Objective	7

Table 12: Survey results on the importance of selected metrics and KPIs

52 TBM Council, 2015

TBM with Apptio

Founded in 2007, Apptio was one of the founding members of the TBM Council in 2012. Apptio is the leader in the TBM market. As a partner to the TBM Council, Apptio is closely involved in creating best practices for TBM. In cooperation with the TBM members, Apptio developed a data model for its TBM technology which fully supports the TBM standard. This data model is known as the Apptio TBM Unified Model or ATUM. It forms the basis for a common understanding of IT costs and provides a standardized cost model for IT organizations. Although company-specific modifications to the ATUM data model are possible, it serves as a good starting point for your TBM journey. It puts you on a path to a successful TBM implementation.

Apptio TBM Solutions

Apptio's offers several TBM solutions in a SaaS delivery model. They cover the following domains:

- Financial Management: Plan, analyze, and optimize technology spend. Accelerate planning cycles, surface spend insights, improve spend decisions.
- Cloud & Hybrid: Manage cloud and hybrid infrastructure. Improve cloud spend visibility, accelerate migration decisions, shape demand with allocation.
- Apps & Services: Rationalize IT services and applications. Measure app & service TCO, identify & prioritize investments, streamline the portfolio.
- Vendors & Suppliers: Manage and monitor vendor spend. Classify & consolidate contracts, control vendor commitments, allocate invoices.
- Agile & Projects: Manage investments in projects. Prioritize portfolio investments, balance demand and capacity, align, and optimize resources.
- Business Value: Communicate and recover costs. Demonstrate business value, track consumption, expose cost, and value levers.

Apptio TBM Products

Apptio's TBM solutions rely on a set of Apptio TBM products domains are supported by several Apptio TBM products, as depicted in Diagram 18:

- Apptio IT Financial Management Foundation: Automate IT financial planning and analysis
- Apptio Cost Transparency: Aggregate and normalize IT cost, increase performance, rationalize IT utilization
- Apptio Cloudability: Optimize and allocate cloud spend and resources
- Apptio Hybrid Business Management: Accelerate cloud migration and optimize hybrid infrastructure
- Apptio Agile Insights: Quantify the business value of agile development
- Apptio Bill of IT: Automate predictable and trustworthy internal billing

In the following section, we will explain three of Apptio's TBM Products in more detail.

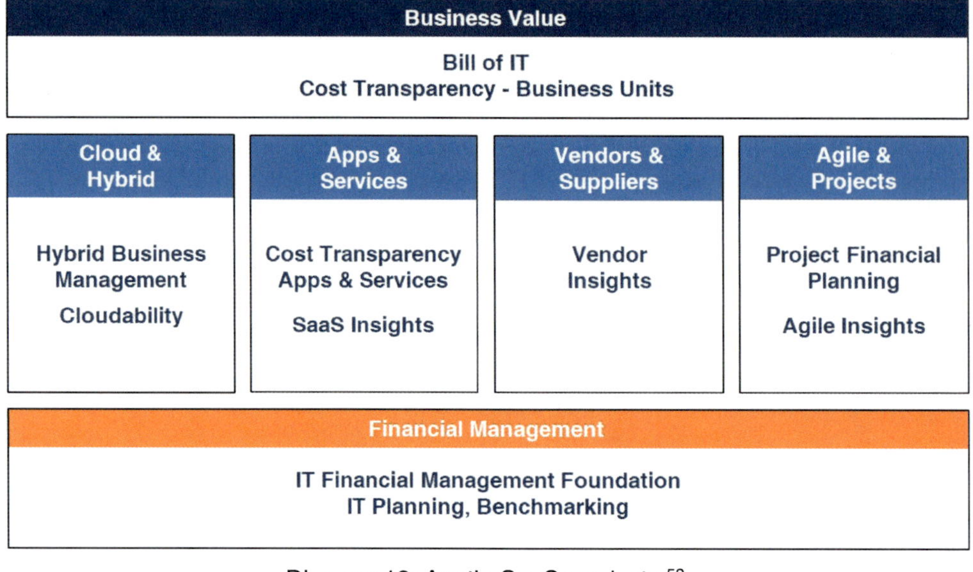

Diagram 18: Apptio SaaS products [53]

Apptio IT Financial Management Foundation

Apptio IT Financial Management Foundation automates and accelerates IT planning and variance analysis, fostering greater accountability, increased plan accuracy, and the agility to free up budget to fund other initiatives. It helps you to

- Increase forecasting frequency to identify shortfalls or overruns faster
- Optimize IT spend and shift funds to fuel digital business innovation.
- Hold budget owners accountable for their spend.

Apptio IT Financial Management Foundation provides you with insights into labor, vendor, and asset spend. It helps you to shift uncommitted spend, optimize the labor mix and roles across departments, consolidate vendor spend and drive economies of scale.

[53] Apptio, 2019

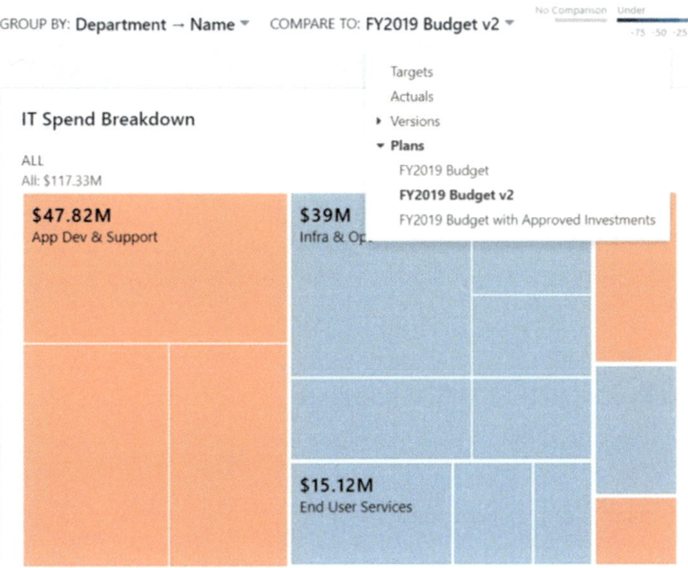

Diagram 19: Spend break down example [54]

You can extend the capabilities of Apptio IT Financial Management Foundation with Apptio Project Financial Planning to shift the focus from organization units (departments) to IT projects. Whether you want to perform budgeting or forecasting with Apptio's IT Planning, the general workflow is the same. It works as follows:

- Budget process owners initiate a plan—be it a budget or a forecast.
- A pre-defined baseline plan is, based on decisions of the planning team, is given to the budget owners.
- Budget owners edit and submit the plan for approval.
- If any approver in the approval chain rejects the plan, it is returned to the respective budget owners to amend and resubmit their plans.
- The budget process owner finalizes plans from all budget owners and rolls them up into the final plan.

You can define the approval hierarchy and the workflow that controls the approval process across the approval hierarchy. Apptio IT Financial Management Foundation supports simplified approvals: e.g., if your department hierarchy included multiple levels, but you would like the approval workflow to be leaner, you can configure it to skip certain levels.

[54] Apptio, 2019

Cost Object	Version in Plan	Status	Last Action	Actions	
▾ All Cost Objects	N/A	In Progress	8/2/19, 8:51 PM	Submit	
CC-200 - Apps - Back Office	Version 1	Returned	7/30/19, 8:58 AM	Comment	
CC-210 - Apps - Line of Business	Version 1	Approved	8/2/19, 8:49 PM	Comment	Return
CC-220 - Apps - Sales & Ops	Version 2	Submitted	8/2/19, 8:51 PM	Comment	Approve
CC-320 - Data Center Ops	Version 1	Submitted	8/2/19, 8:47 PM	Comment	Approve
CC-330 - Network Services	Version 1	Not Started		Comment	Submit
CC-335 - Voice and Call Center	Version 1	Approved	8/2/19, 8:50 PM	Comment	Return
CC-340 - Enterprise Compute & Storage	Version 3	Returned	8/2/19, 8:49 PM	Comment	Submit
CC-345 - Operations Center	Version 1	In Progress	8/2/19, 8:54 PM	Comment	Submit
CC-350 - Service Desk	Version 2	Submitted	8/2/19, 8:50 PM	Comment	Approve
CC-360 - Field Supprt - NA	Version 1	In Progress	8/2/19, 8:52 PM	Comment	Submit
CC-365 - Collaboration & Communication	Version 1	Not Started		Comment	Submit

Diagram 20: Budget processing and approval status [55]

Apptio Cost Transparency

Apptio Cost Transparency automates the analysis of your available IT cost data so you can quickly uncover insights to drive business value.

While cost accounting can be found in other products, Apptio Cost Transparency provides capabilities to calculate defensible service TCO. In our earlier example of the airline check-in service, we demonstrated how hard it is to calculate service TCO accurately—the same applies to the calculation of IT product costs. Apptio Cost Transparency allocates direct and indirect costs to IT services and products by applying various allocation strategies.

Apptio Cost Transparency is where you build your TBM model that controls the flow of cost and defines allocation rules to calculate the total costs of IT services and products—and drives costs along the IT value chain and across the layers of the TBM taxonomy. Cost data is obtained from source systems, undergoes syntactic and semantic transformation, and is categorized into cost pools. From there it is allocated to IT towers, then to IT service and products. Costs are then linked to business capabilities and then, with Apptio Bill of IT, charged to business units.

With Apptio Cost Transparency you

- Make informed decisions from a single system of record.
- Optimize RTB spend to fund future digital business innovation.
- Demonstrate IT value with terms the business understands.

Building your TBM model in Apptio Cost Transparency defines cost flow from a low-level IT resource layer (data centers, software, support, etc.), to a fully-burdened (i.e., inclusive of direct and indirect costs) applications & services layer, and from there up into a business unit layer that consumes IT services.

---

[55] Apptio, 2019

Cost allocation is where IT Finance needs to make a judgment call, and where IT can effectively partner with business consumers of IT. An ideal TBM model helps business unit leaders understand shared costs allocations and build a consensus around the appropriate cost allocation strategies.

Apptio Cost Transparency joins financial and operational data and organizes the data in ATUM. It is comprised of three modules:

- Cost Transparency Foundation: Automates the analysis and reporting on costs by cost pools (e.g., internal labor, vendors, fixed assets), cost centers (IT Towers) on a lower level of the TBM Taxonomy against plan (budget).
- Applications & Services: Automates the analysis and reporting on the TCO of applications and IT services and supports in managing performance against plan (budget).
- Business Units: Automates the analysis and reporting of spend by business unit to understand costs in the context of value and business plans (IT budget allocations).

Module: Cost Transparency Foundation

Cost Transparency Foundation (CTF) starts on the lowest level of the cost structure, organizing costs by cost types and cost pools. After cost data has been obtained from various source systems it is are categorized by fixed and variable costs and then allocated to the Cost Source master table. Costs are allocated based on the following attributes:

- Expenditure type: actual costs or budget
- Fixed or variable costs
- Amount

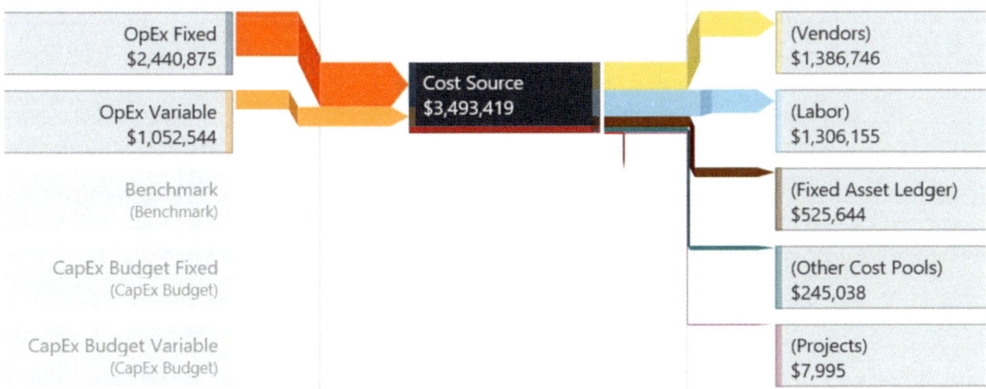

Diagram 21: Cost allocation to and from the Cost Source master table [56]

From the Cost Source master table, costs are allocated to cost pools that are typical for IT organizations:

- Cost of outside services and materials (vendors)

[56] Apptio, 2019

- Costs for internal personnel costs (labor)
- Depreciation of fixed assets (fixed asset ledger)
- Miscellaneous (other cost pools)

The costs for cloud services can be managed at a downstream stage of the cost pool for vendors.

From	Cost Source	Complete
Allocate	All except Budget, CapEx	Complete
Using	Weighted Value	Complete
To	Labor	Complete
Distributing	By Labor Headcount (within Cost_Lab ...	Complete

Diagram 22: Cost allocation by weighted value [57]

Cost data in the Cost Source master table is allocated to the primary cost pools using one of the available allocation methods. From there, costs are allocated to the IT Resource Towers – referring to the IT Towers in the TBM Taxonomy – which represents typical IT organization units.

The IT Resource Tower object is the top of Cost Transparency Foundation. IT Resource Towers are a part of ATUM that translates IT costs into IT functions. IT Resource Towers include functions such as storage, data center, end-user technologies, and compute. IT Resource Towers are typically aligned to cost centers.

For an Apptio novice, this step can be a little confusing as an IT Resource Tower name might be similar to the name of an infrastructure service. You might have an IT Resource Tower that you refer to as "storage" and an IT infrastructure service under the same name: the first refers to the organizational unit that provides expertise on storage technologies, while the second is an IT infrastructure service that provides storage capabilities to other IT services at a defined service level.

The preparatory activities stipulated in the Cost Transparency Foundation module are completed with the allocation of costs to the IT Resource Tower object. From there, move to the Cost Transparency Applications & Services module.

Module: Applications & Services

Once cost data has been allocated to IT Resource Towers it is available for TCO calculations of applications and services as cost objects. The Applications & Services module does not restrict you to a specific TBM model structure. Model your company's specific IT value chain for each IT service and product, and determine how to assign the costs of your IT resources towers to IT Services and products that business units consume.

[57] Apptio, 2019

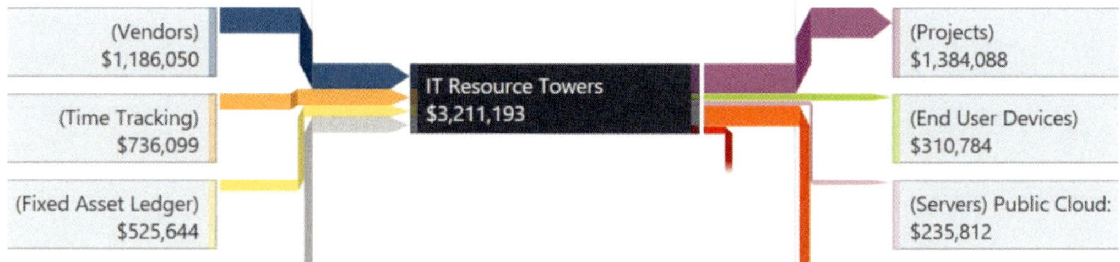

Diagram 23: Cost allocation to the IT Resource Towers information object [58]

Apptio's ATUM follows the TBM Taxonomy of the TBM Council, but the Applications & Services module does not demand pre-defined naming conventions for service categories (i.e., the TBM Taxonomy's naming conventions for infrastructure, platform and business services). While the specifications by the TBM Council are an excellent foundation, Apptio allows room for adaptions.

What additional data do you need?

Look at the allocation of data center costs to other infrastructure costs (e.g., network, server storage components) tracked as IT Resource Towers. You can run the cost allocation by the square meters and rack height units that these components occupy. To do that you, you need consumption data. Here are two examples:

- Storage costs can be allocated to physical servers based on assigned storage volumes.
- Network costs can be allocated to physical servers based on the consumed bandwidth.

You can then conclude that the costs for physical servers consist at a minimum of the direct costs for the server hardware, and a proportion of indirect costs for the data center where the servers are located, the storage assigned to the servers, and network bandwidth used by the servers.

Consumption-based allocations are the fairest. This strategy tracks IT activity that actually happened, as captured in an authoritative system of record, and then uses those numbers to distribute indirect costs.

When calculating the costs of an IT product such as a custom application that your team is developing, you will consider costs for project labor, license costs for off-the-shelf software that might be included in the product, as well as servers and storage for the development and test environments.

When calculating the costs of running an application, consider the costs for the production and disaster recovery environments as well as for delivery services, (e. g., application operation and maintenance). Understand the costs to develop and run an application to compare App Dev vs. App Run—including a view of the full lifecycle costs. Applications that require little investment in the build phase may be very costly in the run phase.

[58] Apptio, 2019

Diagram 24: Allocating costs to applications [59]

IT service costs can be allocated to business services via the number of users in this business unit or other cost drivers such as performance data measured in IT service management Diagram 25 illustrates the cost allocation method for the business services consumed by the business units. The costs of the business services are allocated to a department as follows:

- Costs of business services used exclusively by one business unit are allocated directly as direct costs.
- Costs of business services used by multiple business units are allocated using a cost allocation method (i.e., indirect costs).

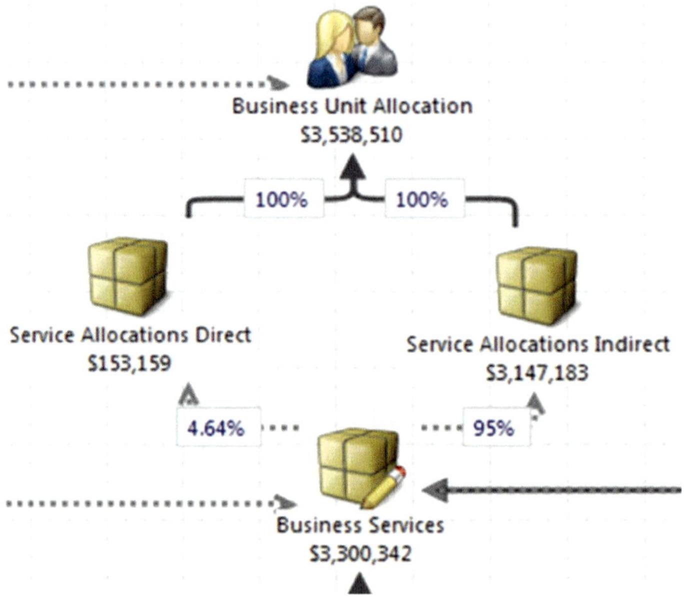

Diagram 25: Indirect and direct allocation of costs to business units [60]

Another example of costs that may directly be passed onto a business unit is the costs of mobile phones and related phone plans. These are assigned, and directly

[59] Apptio, 2019
[60] Apptio, 2019

attributable, to individual employees in the business unit. There is no need to flow these costs through the layer of internal IT services in your model.

All IT costs should be allocated to a business service or an IT product. Unallocated IT cost means unaccountable IT costs. If you find unallocated costs, your team should have a closer look at your service and product portfolio.

Apptio Cloudability

Cloud services provide technological flexibility and scalability as well as "variabilization" of cost. They do not necessarily reduce costs – unless you have the right tools to optimize cloud spend. You can overlook this easily. When adopting cloud service, tight cost control is inevitable.

Understanding and managing the cost of cloud has become a high priority for IT leaders. These costs are highly variable. The ability to spin up cloud services on-demand can lead to ad hoc purchase decisions based on incomplete information. When inadequately monitored or governed, cloud costs skyrocket. There is an increased risk of waste and inefficiency when cloud services are not turned off, or the subscription canceled when no longer needed.

Today, most companies have subscribed to more than one cloud provider - not to mention the various SaaS subscriptions from specialized software vendors. The challenge of cloud cost management must be solved for multiple bills and in different formats. Only then you gain clarity about cloud spend.

One cloud service bill alone can easily consist of thousands of rows and dozens of columns. It is nearly impossible to digest or make sense of the data through manual effort. Apptio provides two products to gain control over cloud costs:

- Apptio Cloudability applies machine learning to optimize cloud resources and translates bills and tags into insights to provide real-time clarity and accountability for consumption.
- Apptio Hybrid Business Management gives IT leaders a single pane of glass to understand, manage and optimize multi-cloud and on-premises infrastructure spend, and accelerate cloud migration.

Daily cloud cost reporting is crucial. Gain real-time visibility into cloud spend to identify and manage irregularities – and then intervene when threshold limits are exceeded. Apptio Cloudability enables you to stay on top of your dynamic cloud spend. See each organizational unit's monthly spend and compare it to the previous months.

An efficient way to reduce cloud spend is to analyze your idle cloud instances. These are quicks wins. Apptio Cloudability identifies instances and quantifies potential cost savings. While production IT services are likely to always run at full capacity, dev and test-related IT services have more leeway and can be switched off during off-hours. If you have employees working on research and development for 10 hours per day only, why run their IT services 24/7? Dedicated reporting on the usage of non-production resources pinpoints when development resources hit peak hours and when they can be scaled back.

Tagging cloud services is a vital way to embed business context into cloud workloads. Without tagging information, cloud provider bills only include information about the provider services and (hopefully) the accounts responsible for deploying the resources. With tagging, you make use of the details. There is a maximum of 50 tags per AWS resource; Azure has a limit of 15 tags per IT services. It is recommended to apply tags directly to the cloud services, rather than depending on a CMDB to connect the dots.

When cloud purchasing is decentralized, establish a policy to have instances that are not fully tagged shut down within 48 hours.

When AWS and Azure generate monthly bills, each of their IT services yields an overwhelming number of billing line items. All of this fidelity is bundled under a single invoice paid each month. Unfortunately, the granularity and meaning are typically lost in cost reporting to IT and business leaders.

With tagging in place, a monthly cloud bill automatically includes tag information for each line of your bill. Here are some examples of tags that will help you to allocate cloud costs within your TBM model:

- Identifier to map the cloud service to the TBM taxonomy.
- Application deployed on the cloud service.
- Environment to which the cloud service is applied e.g., development, test, production.
- Primary user of the cloud service (organizational unit).
- Project associated with the cloud service (project ID).
- Cost Center ID for the financial responsibility of the cloud service.

It is likely that IT leaders will need to manage hybrid IT scenarios even in the distant future. A hybrid IT environment requires a unified model for categorizing cloud and non-cloud costs. Without it, there is no management view of how much cloud spend is going towards storage vs. compute, how much of the enterprise's total compute spend is driven by cloud vs. on-premises implementations, or how cloud is impacting the costs of each IT service that the business consumes.

"Cloud first" does not mean "cloud only". IT leaders will need to manage hybrid IT scenarios even in the distant future. ATUM helps.

By mapping cloud costs to ATUM, you analyze the different cloud service providers based on a common taxonomy. You make apples-to-apples comparisons between cloud and on-premises delivery models.

The full costs of cloud services are not immediately obvious. While you receive detailed billing information from your cloud service providers, you can still lack the full picture. Real cloud costs also include the cost of internal labor, in particular for delivery services. You calculate the cloud TCO as the sum of the costs your cloud service provider charges plus related internal labor cost. You allocate related cost for delivery services to the cost of cloud services.

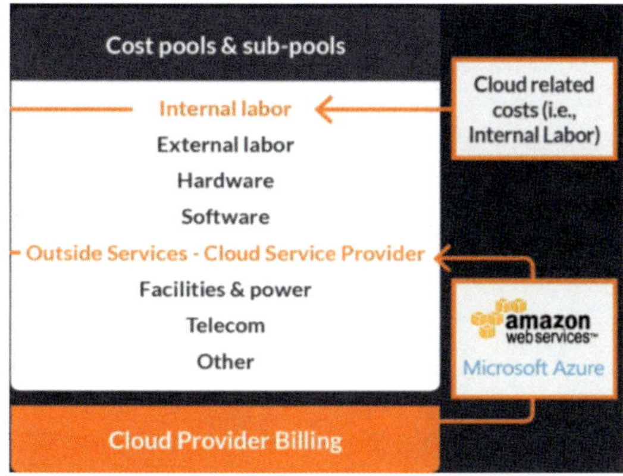

Diagram 26: Calculating the true cost of cloud [61]

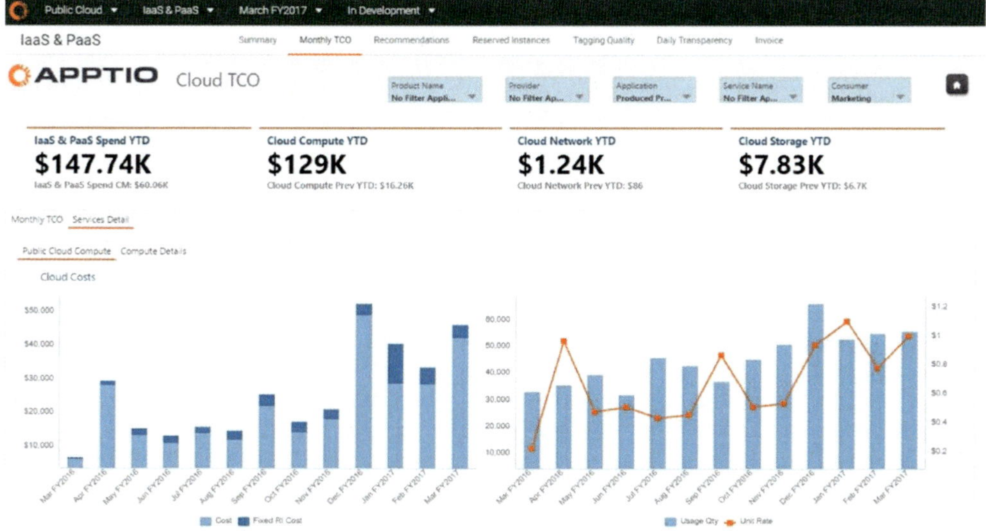

Diagram 27: Understanding the fully-burden Cloud costs [62]

Once you have your cost for cloud services captured you can run additional analysis in Apptio Hybrid Business Management (HBM) and compare cloud services with your and on-premises services. Filter and slice the data by peak utilization to identify underutilized services that can be consolidated.

When analyzing the underlying infrastructure of your on-premises services by age and pulling in assets' lifespan information, focus on servers marked for a refresh. This identifies parts of your infrastructure that are candidates for cloud migration.

HBM delivers the necessary insight to understand the full impact of migration. Before jumping to conclusions too quickly, you want to find some guidance on whether costs can be reduced when replacing on-premises services through cloud services. Current and expected internal costs are compared against the expected cloud

[61] Apptio, 2019
[62] Apptio, 2019

costs based on pricelists from the cloud service providers (AWS, Azure and Google Cloud).

Configuring Apptio to your Needs - TBM Studio

Configure Apptio's TBM solutions and products with TBM Studio. It has three components:

- Apptio Data Studio,
- Apptio Model Studio,
- Apptio Report Studio.

In TBM Studio, configure the loading, transformation, and allocation processes for cost and activity data. It is also where you create TBM reports and dashboards. The logic of handling data and formulas in both is comparable with Microsoft Excel. TBM Studio is a better choice for a TBM implementation—it sets a focus on processing IT cost and activity data.

Diagram 28 shows the flow of cost and activity data in Apptio solution architecture. Data is loaded form source systems, then transformed and assigned to the master data sets. From there it feeds into a company-specific cost model and finally into reports.

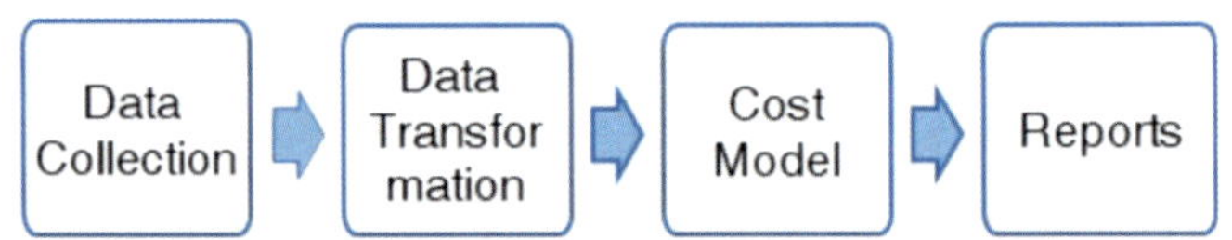

Diagram 28: Data flow from the source systems to the reports [63]

Apptio offers its software as a service (SaaS). This takes the pain out of setting up the required infrastructure and installing the software on premises. The software is provided on different environments to configure, test and operate TBM applications:

- development environment,
- staging environment,
- production environment.

As you configure your TBM solution, you first check out components on the development environment to work on them. The label "development environment" might be misleading as the work that is required is mostly configuration work. After having configured individual application components you release them to the staging environment for testing and eventually to the production environment. The whole process is clear. At any point in time, you and other team members see which components are checked out and being worked on.

Apptio Data Studio

An Apptio application uses data from company-internal source systems and external sources such as Amazon AWS or Microsoft Azure. The data can automatically

[63] Apptio, 2014

be fetched form the source systems through Apptio's Datalink connectors. You can set a frequency of how often the data shall be refreshed, new data is uploaded respectively.

When data is syntactical and semantically not aligned, configure loading and transformation processes in Apptio Data Studio. Build transformation pipelines, which hold the rules to fetch data and align and load into Apptio's master data sets. Defining a transformation pipeline is simple. Determine which tables to use and apply one or multiple transformation steps. Apptio Data Studio provides an overview of all transformation steps. This makes debugging fairly easy.

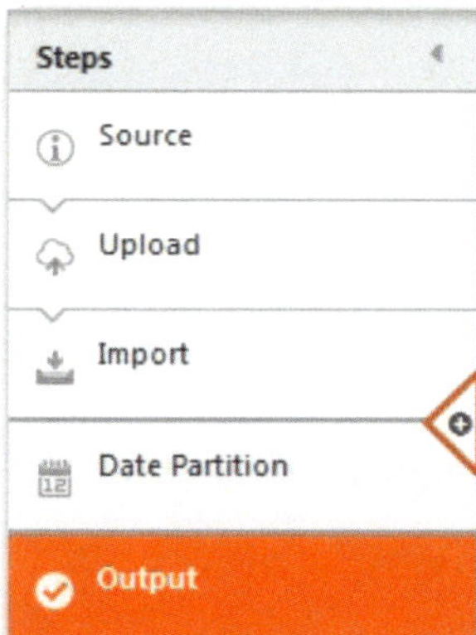

Diagram 29: Example of an Apptio transformation pipeline [64]

Apptio Data Studio shows transform steps in the order they are executed. You can create, edit, and delete transform steps as well as change the order of the steps and preview the data at each step. Table 13 shows examples of Data Studio's basic data transformation functions.

Basic Transformation Functions	Description
Filter	Filters out rows of data based on one or multiple filter rules.
Group	Groups rows of data by one or multiple columns.
Remove Duplicates	Removes duplicate entries in a table based on values in a selected column.
Append	Appends rows of data to a master or another dataset in the system by mapping the columns.
Hide, Rename	Hides or renames columns of data for the subsequent transform pipeline steps.

Table 13: Basic transformation functions

Apptio Data Studio offers more advanced functions including:

- join function to combine data from two or more tables into the same rows based on common values in one or more columns.

[64] Apptio, 2019

- date partition function to assign data to time periods based on time stamps.
- flatten hierarchy function to break down hierarchical table by adding columns to table, one column for each level in the hierarchy.
- cleanse function to ensure that data meets the standards for integrity, conformity, and completeness.

Apptio Data Studio handles necessary data loading and transformation tasks. After transformation, you release the data with an output function to defined tables in the Apptio data model.

ATUM

The Apptio TBM Unified Model (ATUM®) standardizes the financial information necessary for IT leaders to manage their technology business. Apptio applications are based on ATUM's standard cost model for IT costs. It consists of master data sets that stipulate data formats and how the data is organized. Master data sets distinguish required and optional attributes. After data has been loaded and transformed, it is assigned to the respective attributes of the master data sets.

Apptio Data Advisor checks the completeness of the data from the source systems. It identifies missing attributes. Below are examples of the Apptio's master data sets. For a complete set refer to Apptio's Data Advisor tool.

- Applications
- Cloud Service Providers
- Data Centers
- Hypervisors
- Physical Server
- Projects
- Servers
- Storage
- Tickets
- Vendors

One of the first steps in assigning data to master data sets is to map data from the accounts in your general ledger to cost pools. Previously, this required a manual mapping of files with one-by-one assignments to reach the taxonomy-standard cost pools. Apptio automates this step. Adjustments can still be made after the process has been completed. It is the work of a TBM analyst who checks the assignments.

Apptio Model Studio

Configure your TBM model with Apptio Model Studio. The model controls the flow of cost, budget and quantity data. It holds the allocation rules to calculate TCO for IT services and products. It drives costs along the IT value chain and across the different ATUM layers.

The model determines the allocation path of cost from the general ledger, cost pools, IT towers, and services. Service costs can then be assigned to specific products. Apply cost drivers to flow data through the model—from one object to one or more other objects. Apptio provides several diagram types to visualize models. The following is an example of a Sankey diagram [65] with applied cost allocation methods.

[65] Sankey, H., 1896

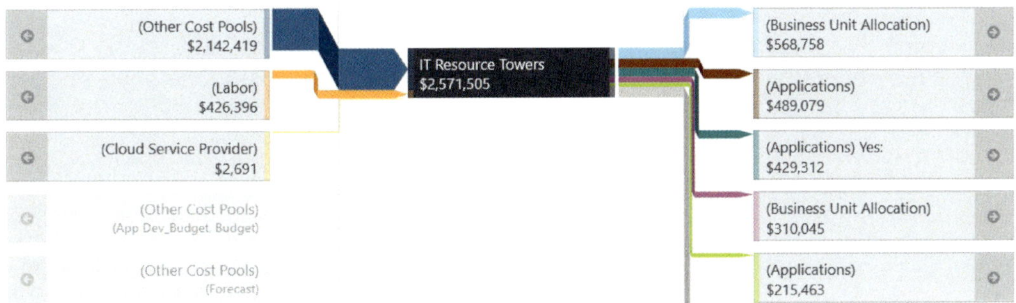

Diagram 30: Sankey diagram with cost allocations [66]

One of the most powerful features in Apptio Model Studio is the definition of allocation schemes. Apptio supports the following allocation methods:

- Weighted Value allocations
- Consumption allocations
- Standard Value allocations
- Formula allocations
- Recursion allocations

Apptio's Model Reports displays the full IT value chain while allowing for analysis on individual cost elements. Let's say you want to explain how costs are driven from cost pools to IT resource towers to services and to business units, then a Model Report is your best choice.

Diagram 31: Section of a model report [67]

The tiers in an Apptio Model Studio model report can focus on a single cost attribute only. This is helpful if you want to perform analysis on the level of an individual element such as a specific cost pool only.

A model not only determines cost allocations across the various ATUM layers but populates metrics. There are two types of metrics:

- Modeled metrics. A model is itself a metric. A model calculates a numeric value such as cost, quantity, or budget.

[66] Apptio, 2019
[67] Apptio, 2019

- Calculated metrics. A calculated metric uses a formula to derive a numeric value. For example, you could create a calculated metric called Budget_Variance defined as the Budget modeled metric minus the Cost modeled metric.

Metrics are used to perform variance analysis, e.g., to show how operational data such as the availability relates to the TCO of an IT service. Important metrics are referred to as key performance indicators (KPIs). Diagram 32 depicts a modeled metric.

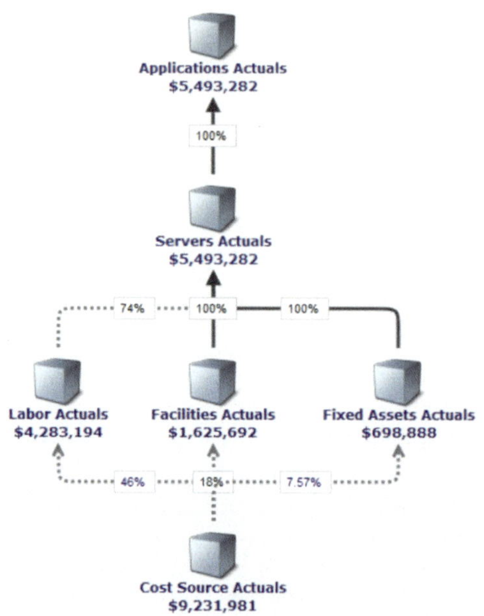

Diagram 32: Modeled metric [68]

Apptio Report Studio

Apptio Report Studio is where you create reports and dashboards to present insights. It comes with preconfigured, customizable reports. Adjustments are performed through drag & drop and selecting appropriate items from picklists. Providing reports is achievable without programming skills. Out-of-the-box reports offer role-specific insights for CIOs, account managers, service managers etc. Access rights to reports can be assigned for each report—stakeholders see the information they have the right to see.

Apptio Report Studio offers many predefined standard tables that can quickly be added to reports. Most of them specifically cater to the needs of IT cost management. Here are some examples:

- Use an Inference Match table to show how closely the units in a model objects match a common concept. The higher the percentage, the better the value of the object can be allocated.

[68] Apptio, 2019

- Apply an Assignments table to list the unit IDs of each target object and to show the value allocated to each of the units from the source object.
- Include a Profit and Loss table to analyze the cost flows to and from objects in the middle layers of your cost model. The table displays the allocations at the unit level and summarizes them in a profit and loss figure. If inflow and outflow are equal, the net profit and loss will be zero.

Apptio Report Studio offers slicers, field pickers, and quick pivots. Slicers filter tables or charts by selected values. They set the focus on specific elements and reveals insights that might be overlooked otherwise. Field pickers add columns, and quick pivots group the data by a selected column.

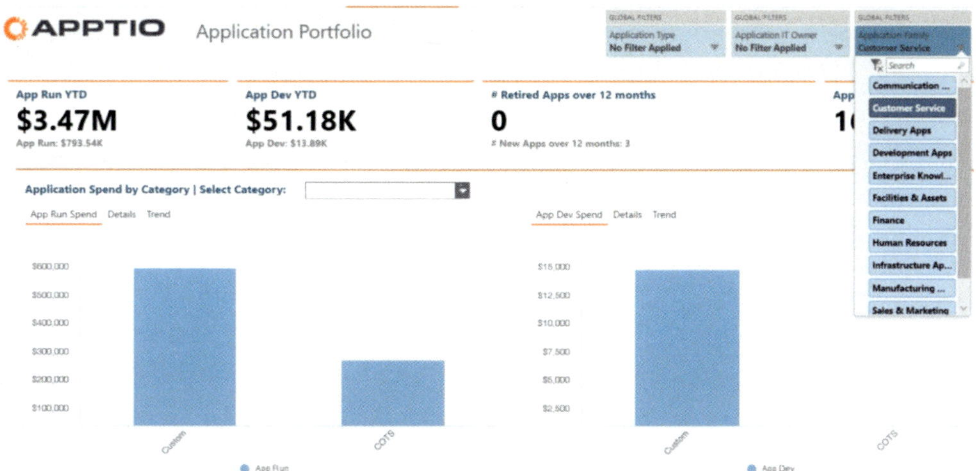

Diagram 33: Applied filter in a report [69]

Report designers use the component configuration panel to build the tables and charts in a report. They drag fields from Apptio's Project Explorer into the report panel (e.g., define the rows and columns of a table structure as well as which values to show and filters to apply). Use a report collections group to group reports that cover a similar topic. Users navigate between these reports.

Apptio Report Studio offers the cutting-edge features that you would expect e.g., zooming in on charts by holding down the mouse button and dragging the mouse pointer horizontally across a chart or drill-down features in tables and charts to get more details about individual elements.

[69] Apptio, 2019

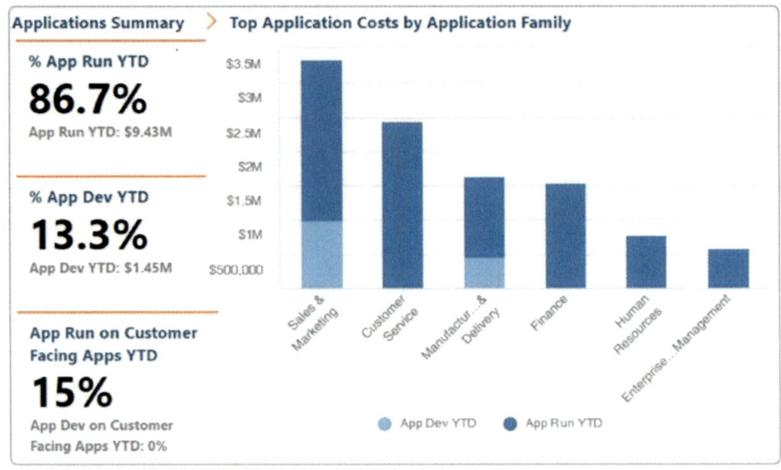

Diagram 34: Dashboard component – application dev vs. run costs [70]

[70] Apptio, 2019

Start Your TBM Journey

Dr. Fochler & Company (www.fochler.com) helps clients transform their IT operating model through TBM. We have a solid set of activities that get your organization to achieve benefits quickly.

Transforming an organization is not easy; it requires an organizational and behavioral change for both IT and business units. Just like any successful transformation, TBM adoption demands a disciplined approach with program management, dedicated resources, and sufficient funding.

We will jointly enter your TBM journey with you.

Let's start with the development of a TBM strategy that articulates the vision, objectives, and expected outcomes when transforming your IT organization. The strategy offers a plan to move your organization from its current state to the desired target state. During your TBM journey, we will support you in:

- Assessing the TBM readiness of your organization regarding data, process, people, communications, and metrics. Securing sponsorship at the executive level. Achieving engagement from the business and finance units.
- Calculating the business case for TBM adoption, determining implementation and lifecycle cost and quantifying benefits.
- Automating budgeting and forecasting to simulate the impact of alternative business strategies on IT costs.
- Verifying your IT Service catalog for completeness: Listing business, infrastructure and delivery services with relevant service attributes, e.g., provisioning times, service levels etc.
- Building cost models for each service including allocation of direct and indirect costs as well as the determining the best cost drivers. Calculating unit costs for infrastructure services as commodities for benchmarking against peers and public cloud service offerings.
- Rationalizing IT service and vendor portfolios by ranking them according to value and performance.
- Shifting IT budgets to technology innovations by optimizing IT run cost and freeing budget to equip your company's business model with cutting-edge technologies.

Now you have the content and context to start the transformation of your IT operating model. It's time to have the conversation.

Contact us at team@fochler.com

References

Aljaber, T. (2019): The Iron Triangle of Planning. At Atlassian Agile Coach: www.atlassian.com/agile/agile-at-scale/agile-iron-triangle.

Amazon (2019): AWS Total Cost of Ownership (TCO) Calculator. https://aws.amazon.com: https://awstcocalculator.com.

Apptio (2014): ATUM Whitepaper.

Apptio (2016): Partner Demo. Understand & Communicate IT Value.

Apptio (2017): Cost Transparency Foundation Configuration Guide R12.

Apptio (2019): About Models. Von TBM Connect. https://tbmcouncil.jiveon.com/docs/DOC-4891.

Apptio (2019): TBM Studio 12.7 Data Studio Guide. TBM Connect. https://tbmcouncil.jiveon.com/docs/DOC-11717.

Atlassian (2019): DevOps: Breaking the Development-Operations barrier. www.atlassian.com: www.atlassian.com/devops.

Bragg, S. (2017): www.accountingtools.com. https://www.accountingtools.com/articles/2017/5/14/activity-based-costing.

Kaplan, R. S., Bruns, W. (1987): Accounting and Management: A Field Study Perspective. Harvard Business School Press.

Keys, D. E., van der Merwe, A. (1999): Germany vs. United States Cost Management. Management Accounting Quarterly.

Krumwiede, K., Suessmair, A. (2007): Comparing U.S. and German Cost Accounting Methods. Management Accounting Quarterly, S. Vol. 8 No. 3.

Law, J. (1705): Money and Trade Consisdered. Edinburgh, Scotland.

Lindenthaler, B. (2008): IT-Services und ASP: Design und Erstellung eines Service-Katalogs für Application Service Provider. Vienna, Austria: Master Thesis, University of Vienna.

Ryan, R., Raducha-Grace, T. (2009): Business of IT, The: How to Improve Service and Lower Costs. IBM Press.

Ryan, R., Raducha-Grace, T. (2009): informit.com. IT Financial Management. The Business of IT. http://www.informit.com/articles/article.aspx?p=1397671

Sankey, H. P. (1896): The Thermal Efficiency of Steam-Engines. M.P.I.C.E.

Staubus, G. J. (1971): Activity Costing and Input-Output Accounting. Richard D. Irwin, Inc.

Staubus, G. J. (1971): Activity Costing and Input-Output Accounting .

TBM Council (2015): Survey: TBM Council Board Meeting. Yountville, CA, USA.

TBM Council (2018): TBM Taxonomy, Version 3.0.

The IFRS Foundation (2019). IFRS. https://www.ifrs.org/

TSO (2011): ITIL Service Strategy. Belfast, Ireland.

Tucker, T. (2016): Technology Business Management. Technology Business Management Council, Ltd.

Wikipedia (2019): Cost Accounting. https://en.wikipedia.org/wiki/Cost_accounting

Wikipedia (2019): Taxonomy. https://en.wikipedia.org/wiki/Taxonomy.

Made in the USA
Monee, IL
30 December 2019

19688980R00043